Other books by Richard E. Nicholls
published by Running Press

The Plant Doctor:
  Growing and Healing Indoor Plants

The Handmade Greenhouse:
  From Windowsill to Backyard

The Plant Doctor in His Vegetable Garden:
  A Beginner's Handbook

The Plant Buyer's Handbook:
  A Consumer's Guide to Buying House Plants

The Running Press Book of
TURTLES

by Richard E. Nicholls

Color Illustration by Verlin Miller

Running Press
Philadelphia, Pennsylvania

Distributed in Canada by Van Nostrand Reinhold, Ltd., Ontario, Canada. International representatives: Kaimon & Polon, Inc., 456 Sylvan Avenue, Englewood Cliffs, New Jersey 07632.

9   8   7   6   5   4   3   2   1
Digit on right indicates the number of this printing.

Library of Congress Cataloging in Publication Data

Nicholls, Richard, 1949-
  The Running Press Book of Turtles.
  Bibliography: p. 145.
  Includes index.
  SUMMARY: Describes the physical characteristics and behavior of various North American turtles and discusses their relationship to humans in myth and reality. Also includes information on caring for turtles as pets.
  1. Turtles—North America. 2. Reptiles—North America. [1. Turtles.
2. Reptiles] I. Title. II. Title: Turtles.
QL666.C5N53   598.1'3   77-4413
ISBN: 0-914294-86-5 Paperback
ISBN: 0-914294-85-7 Library binding

Running Press wishes to thank the following for permission to reproduce from their publications:

   From *The Outermost House* by Henry Beston. Copyright 1928, 1949, © 1956 by Henry Beston. Reprinted by permission of Holt, Rinehart and Winston, publishers.
   Reprinted from Archie Carr: *Handbook of Turtles.* © 1952 by Cornell University. Used by permission of Cornell University Press.
   Turtles of the United States by Carl H. Ernst and Roger W. Barbour. Copyright © 1972 by The University Press of Kentucky.
   From *Rolf in the Woods*, by Ernest Thompson Seton. © 1911 by Ernest Thompson Seton. Reprinted by permission of Doubleday & Company, Inc., and Anya Seton Chase.
   Verse translation in "Epilogue" courtesy of the Rio Grande Classic Edition of *The Last of the Seris*, © The Rio Grande Press, Inc., Glorieta, New Mexico.
   Illustrations in Chapter 6 courtesy of the Dover Pictorial Archive Series, Dover Publications, Inc., New York.

Cover and interior color illustrations by Verlin Miller
Cover design by Jim Wilson
Interior art direction by Linda Grossman
Edited by Peter J. Dorman

Typography: Caledonia, by The Kingswood Group, Ardmore, Pennsylvania
Cover printed by Harrison Color Process Lithographers, Willow Grove, Pennsylvania
Interior color plates printed by Schawkgraphics, Inc., Chicago, Illinois
Printed and bound by Port City Press, Baltimore, Maryland

This book may be ordered directly from the publisher.
Please include 25 cents postage.

Try your bookstore first.

Running Press
38 South Nineteenth Street
Philadelphia, Pennsylvania 19103

Premise

Turtles were here before us.

Here, in North America, when the continent was still being formed by the ceaseless actions of ice, wind, and wave.

Here, in this world, when the dinosaurs appeared, here while they dominated life, and here when the dinosaurs failed and became extinct.

And here they have remained. Surviving all the upheavals of nature. Surviving, so far, the great disruptions and changes that the upstart humans have worked on the world.

This is no matter of chance or mere good fortune. Turtles have made it through so much because they are tough, adaptable creatures, the champions of a long evolutionary process which has molded flexible patterns of behavior in conformity with a unique body design.

Turtles have survived the many dangers of the natural world; and they have prospered. Whether they will survive the great difficulties now confronting them depends as much on the actions of us humans as on the turtles themselves. By understanding how remarkable these creatures are, *we* can take a first step toward helping them maintain their place, and their pace, in the world.

v

List of Color Plates

Plate I   Eastern Painted Turtle
Chrysemys picta picta

Plate II   Red-Eared Turtle
Chrysemys scripta elegans

Plate III   Florida Box Turtle
Terrapene carolina bauri

Plate IV   Northern Diamondback Terrapin
Malaclemys terrapin terrapin

Plate V   Yellow-Bellied Turtle
Chrysemys scripta scripta

Plate VI   Yellow Mud Turtle
Kinosternon flavescens flavescens

Plate VII   Wood Turtle
Clemmys insculpta

Plate VIII   Eastern Mud Turtle
Kinosternon subrubrum subrubrum

Plate IX   Southern Painted Turtle
Chrysemys picta dorsalis

Plate X   Map Turtle
Graptemys geographica

Plate XI   Alabama Map Turtle
Graptemys pulchra

Plate XII   The Life Cycle of Turtles

Plate XIII   Eastern Box Turtle
Terrapene carolina carolina

Contents

Premise v
List of Color Plates vi
Introduction ix

PART ONE: TURTLES THEMSELVES

Chapter 1   The Body Is the Plan 15
The Shell • In and Around the Shell • Perception and
Intelligence

Chapter 2   Courtship, Mating, and Reproduction 27
The Sex Life of Fresh-Water Turtles • The Nest, the Egg, and
the Hatchling • The Loves of the Sea Turtle

Chapter 3   Habitat and Behavior 37
The Oceans • The Marshlands • Fresh-Water Habitats • The
Woodlands • Deserts: The Desert Tortoise • The Prairies •
On Observing Turtles in Their Natural Habitats • Species of
North American Turtles • Portfolio of Color Plates

PART TWO: TURTLES AND PEOPLE

Chapter 4   Exploitation by Homo Sapiens 93
Hunting in the Amazon • The Miskito: A Cautionary Tale •
The Uses of the Sea Turtle • North American Fare: Diamond-
backs and Snappers • Technology Versus Turtles • The
Galapagos Tortoise

Chapter 5   Caring for Turtles as Pets 111
Shopping for Turtles • On Keeping Turtles: Environment and
Food • Keeping Terrestrial Turtles Outdoors • Keeping Fresh-
Water Turtles Outdoors • Keeping Fresh-Water Turtles
Indoors • Keeping Terrestrial Turtles Indoors • Diseases and
Cures • It Followed Me Home

Chapter 6   On Turtle Island 133
Chinese Mythology • Central American Folklore • North
American Indian Tales

Epilogue 142
Bibliography 145
Index 149

Dedication

This book is dedicated, with thanks, to all those who have generously shared their knowledge of turtles with the author. It is also dedicated, with admiration, to all those who are laboring to save the turtles from extinction.

Introduction

"Tortois, vulgarly called Turtle: I have ranked them among the Insects, because they lay eggs, and I did not know well where to put them."

So wrote the perplexed John Lawlor, in an inventory of New World creatures published in his book *The History of North Carolina*, issued in London in 1712. Since then, although there has been a tremendous amount of research done on the turtles, little of it has found its way into general circulation. Turtles are still, so far as many people are concerned, rather dull, uninteresting creatures, relegated to an anonymity almost as great as that we accord to the faceless insects. Many of us still know almost as little about turtles and tortoises as poor John Lawlor.

It is my intention in this book to undermine that common image, and to further its replacement by a true image of a remarkable and unjustly ignored creature. When I began researching this book, my own knowledge of turtles was none too thorough. I had the conviction that turtles were a good deal more interesting than they were usually thought to be, but I would have been hard pressed to cite the facts to prove my conviction. In a sense, this book is the result of that search, a record of my encounter with the chelonians.

It has not been my intention to cover in an exhaustive manner all facets of the turtle's structure, behavior, and habitat. A large body of scientific literature now exists on North American species. There are several superb books, including one by Clifford Pope, one by Archie Carr, and another by Carl Ernst and Roger Barbour, that provide an exhaustive review of all the known facts about each of the species and subspecies. These books are cited in the Bibliography. I have attempted to introduce the most salient points about the turtles, to incorporate the most exciting discoveries about their structure, behavior, and relations to their habitat: in short, to present a case for regarding and treating turtles in a more positive manner.

I have laid special stress on this matter of treatment, for the record of our interactions with turtles has been generally bad, and sometimes devastating. Decimating species for food, flattening, filling in and paving over their habitats, or taking them in massive numbers for the pet trade, our effect has always been disruptive. We have done the most damage by ignoring turtles, by treating them as if they were of no consequence, and thus not to be taken into account. Frequently we have endangered species of turtles without much caring about it, unwilling to take those steps necessary to preserve them, their habitats and thus, indirectly, the quality of our own lives. When we casually allow bodies of water to be badly polluted, or marshes to be filled in, prairies and woodlands to be torn out, used up, paved over, we are diminishing the health of our environment, and ultimately our own health and resiliency of mind and spirit.

Finally, I have presented turtles as examples, in and of themselves, of the ways in which a creature can adapt to, and live in, habitats in a harmonious manner—and, as examples of the ways in which we thoughtlessly abuse other forms of life.

It is my hope that this book will serve as a first step, encouraging you to begin seeing turtles, and, more generally, all other creatures, as something more than automatons, faceless, selfless things to be used as food, sport, or a passing source of amusement. For if you can begin to *see* another creature— really see it as worthy of respect, as a unique, successful being—your ways of treating it and the world around you must improve. It is only what we don't know, or don't try to know, that we can use in an unconscientious manner. We (most of us) don't know turtles, and it is past time that we did. May this book, then, serve as your introduction.

A Note on Terminology

Turtles are classified by herpetologists as being members of the zoological subclass Anapsida, within which they constitute an order of their own, the Testudines, or shelled reptiles. This order is then divided into two suborders, the Pleurodira and Cryptodira. The two suborders have together a total of twelve families. The species of North American turtles represent seven of these families: the Chelydridae (snapping turtles); Kinosternidae (mud, musk turtles); Emydidae (aquatic, semiaquatic, box turtles); Testudinidae (desert, gopher tortoises); Cheloniidae (sea turtles); Dermochelyidae (leatherback turtle); and the Trionychidae (softshell turtles). All of the species found in North America, or in the waters around it, are members of the suborder Cryptodira. This classification and Latinate terminology make it possible for scientists throughout the world to talk about turtles in a shared language, which everywhere means the same thing. Only in this way can considerable confusion be avoided.

That it is possible for terms to be given different meanings in different locations is very evident in the confusion over common names for turtles. In England, the word *turtle* is still generally used only to refer to sea turtles. All non-sea-going turtles are called *tortoises*. However, in the United States the word tortoise is used to refer only to those species that live most of the time on land (desert tortoises, for instance). All of the species that live in fresh-water habitats, or that are sea-going, are known as turtles. Indeed, in common parlance almost every species of chelonian is referred to as a turtle. An American reading a book on chelonians published in England would likely be somewhat perplexed.

In this book I follow American usage. All species living primarily in or around bodies of fresh water, and all sea-going species, are referred to as turtles. Species living most of the time on the land are referred to as tortoises. In addition, I use the terms *aquatic, terrestrial,* and *marine* to further identify the species: an aquatic species lives in fresh water; a terrestrial species lives on the land; and a marine species lives in the sea. The word *chelonian,* originally derived from the zoological name for the sea turtles (exclusive of the leatherback), has now entered the language as a term used to refer in general to turtles and tortoises, or to anything pertaining to them. As it provides some break in the repetition of common names, and as I am rather fond of the word, I have used it frequently in the text.

Richard E. Nicholls

—Richard E. Nicholls

PART I
Turtles Themselves

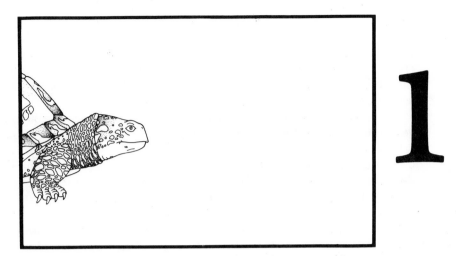

The Body Is the Plan

Throughout its evolutionary march toward an existence safe from ferocious predators in a hard and uncertain world, the turtle underwent one of the most thoroughgoing transformations of any species of reptile living or dead. Every aspect of its body was modified to suit the creature's needs for food and shelter. While similar adaptations can be traced among other species, few can claim so many critical changes. And few have been around so long to claim them.

No one can say just how long turtles have been present in the marshes, rivers, forests, prairies, and deserts of North America, or inhabited the seas bordering the continent. Indeed, it is impossible to say within a range of less than a few million years when the first turtle deserving of the name appeared. Nor is the evolutionary process by which some species of reptiles developed into turtles altogether clear. There are few clues in the fossil record by which the evolution of turtles can be traced, and those few are open to a variety of interpretations. Whatever the interpretations, the outcome of all the changes is the well-planned body of the turtle living today.

Turtles are descendants of the primitive cotylosaurs, or "stem" reptiles, as are all species of reptiles living and extinct. Evolving from amphibians some 250 million years ago, these stem reptiles (now extinct) were the first creatures capable of living permanently on the marshy fingers of the continent. While a variety of amphibians had been shuttling between water and land for some time, their visits were limited by the effects of sunlight and air on unprotected skin. Exposed to the drying power of the elements, amphibians would rapidly become dehydrated; if they were not nimble in returning to the seas, they would perish. They could not produce young on the land, for the elements would quickly destroy their unshielded, watery egg masses, cooking them into a thin layer of paste. The cotylosaurs overcame these problems by developing scales and shelled eggs: both innovations served to protect them from the elements by giving relative freedom of movement in and out of the water—a freedom greater than any other creature had previously attained. The success of the cotylosaurs in settling on the continents made all things possible: from them flows the entire astonishing pantheon of reptiles, including the turtles.

There may have been turtles, or proto-turtles, as long ago as 200 million years. However, the fossil record for this period is incomplete and frequently confusing. Opinion is divided as to whether the *Eunotosaurus africanus*, a small reptile appearing about that time, is or is not an ancestor of the turtles. Although its eight wide ribs suggest the presence of a shell, its remains are so scanty that paleontologists cannot wholly reconstruct what it looked like.

Whatever intermediate chelonian forms might have evolved, turtles had emerged as distinct, and very different, species of reptiles by the onset of the Cretaceous period some 140 million years ago, a geologic period marked by the proliferation of flowering plants and the gradual extinction of giant predatory reptiles such as the dinosaurs. During this age turtles are very much in evidence in many portions of the world, indicating the success of their form. And while the fossil record is still far from being either very broad or deep, it does present a strong case for viewing the turtle as a creature common to many regions of the still-developing world. There have been instances when paleontologists, seeking out the bones of rare reptilian species in diverse locations, have found what they were seeking covered by, even encased in, thick layers of jumbled turtle bones.

These first true turtles, like their ancestors the cotylosaurs, were almost certainly marsh dwellers. The marshes provided an environment still sufficiently watery for creatures only recently removed from a sea-going life, while the knobs of land found throughout the marshes provided exposure to the possibilities of a terrestrial life. Perhaps the turtles, and many other species, might have remained in the marshes, becoming more and more specialized as marsh dwellers, had not periodic droughts withered the marshy habitats. Driven by the failure of this known world to support them, the turtles moved inland, carefully probing the opportunities for survival in forests, ponds, rivers, prairies, and even deserts. At some unknown point, certain species of turtles re-entered the seas which their distant progenitors had left; and there they stayed, retaining only the need to lay their eggs ashore.

The Shell

That turtles successfully adapted to a wide variety of environments, and were frequently present in great numbers, makes good evolutionary sense. They had achieved a degree of invulnerability possessed by few other creatures. And they had done this by the fortuitous development of one feature: a shell: a highly specialized structure integrated with the body and

16

symbolic of the turtle's remarkable adaptability. Several theories have been advanced to explain how the shelled animal came into being. One suggests a turtle-like ancestor having flexible, hard plates of skin along its back. When threatened, the creature would roll itself into an armored ball, behaving much like the armadillo now found commonly in the American Southwest. Another theory, put forward by the eminent herpetologist Archie Carr, calls for a series of changes leading towards the shell as a development of the defense reaction common to many animals in which the shoulders are hunched and the back bowed, allowing the vulnerable head to be drawn out of the reach of sharp teeth and sharper claws.

The principal pressure behind the development of the shell was survival. The turtle entered a world filled with scores of species of large, powerful predators, the dinosaurs. Had the immediate ancestors of the turtle failed to develop a tough shell (or shell-like structure), it is unlikely that they would have survived. The shell, while it could resist the pressure of all but the most determined attack, was most important in discouraging any notion of attack. Having learned that the turtle presented hard work with little reward, predators logically turned to other, more tender prey.

It is by its shell that the turtle is known: the creature and its most obvious physical characteristic are inseparable in our thoughts. This is not unusual—we often catalog a creature for our memory by connecting its name with some outstanding physical feature, characteristic, or behavior. (*Testudinidae*, a taxonomic Family name of turtles, contains the Latin root *testa* meaning "head," "pot," and "shell.") The turtle is unique in that its shell has served, at least since people began thinking and writing about turtles, as a symbol of the creature's mode of life: as a concept of survival exemplified in the flesh. In no other animal, I think, do we find a better fusion of idea and form, of form and function.

The achievement of the turtle, however, is quite easily misread. Having once shaped its body into a refuge, the turtle is represented as a profoundly conservative creature, being either unable or unwilling to change. Such is not the case. Many species of turtles have undergone radical alterations of behavior in adapting to many different environments, whereas other species incapable of adjusting to changing conditions have failed and become extinct, joining the thousands of species of reptiles and mammals that have developed, become dominant, and disappeared over the ages. The concept of the shell as a solution to every sort of problem is mistaken. In and of itself a shell cannot assure survival. It is important only as it is utilized in handling diverse needs and conditions, and as a symbol of what a species is capable of doing to survive. The turtle makes the shell, and not the shell the turtle.

If they retain any ancestral memory, turtles must surely remember the passing of many species, great and small, who mastered the lessons of existence only imperfectly and became extinct. Such failed creatures, out of what one imagines as complacency or arrogance, proved unable to master the knowledge turtles have passed on for more than 100 million years: *adapt or perish.* Given all that they have witnessed, it would not be surprising to find, as Archie Carr has suggested, that over the eons turtles have taken in stride the activities of "a mob of irresponsible and shifty-eyed little shrews [who] swarmed down out of the trees to chip at stones, and fidget around fires, and build atom bombs." (P. 4.)

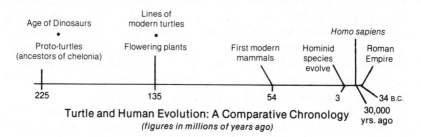

Turtle and Human Evolution: A Comparative Chronology
(figures in millions of years ago)

While the primary function of the shell is obvious to the most casual observer, its construction is frequently misunderstood. People never having had the opportunity to closely examine a turtle might imagine that the shell is somewhat like a permanent suit of armor, an external covering unattached to the soft body crouching within. I remember that as a child I was rather perplexed by the antics of a cartoon turtle which was prone to leap from its shell when danger threatened, leaving the empty shell behind to baffle its assailants as it dashed away.

A turtle cannot shrug off its shell, nor does it have a stout body independent of its covering. The turtle is one with its shell: the shell is the outer layer of its being. Fused with the shell are the turtle's bones, and suspended beneath it are its organs. It cannot ever leave its shell, just as we cannot step outside of our skin.

The terminology describing the various parts of a turtle's shell is complex and lengthy, but it is worth mentioning to point up the remarkably intricate nature of the shell's design. Although it is potentially misleading to discuss parts that are fused together as if they were separate, it does bring clarity to the subject.

The shell of a turtle is composed of two pieces: the carapace, forming the top, and the plastron, forming the bottom. These pieces meet along the turtle's midsection where they are connected on each side by lateral bridges of shell that leave openings between the front and back portions of the carapace and plastron. Through these open spaces the head, limbs, and tail of the turtle protrude. The openings provide great freedom of movement and make it possible for a turtle to withdraw its head, a vitally important defense mechanism.

The carapace and plastron are each composed of two closely connected layers: the innermost thick plates of bone and the outermost horny raised plates known as laminae. The plates of bone developed through a modification and fusion of the ribs and back vertebrae (the bone plates are the turtle's equivalent of ribs). This fusion of parts in the creation of a portable "house" of bones has called for a major sacrifice: a turtle is safe, but it is not supple. The spine is fixed and immovable; its only moving parts are the neck and tail bones. The breastbone and collarbone, present in other rep-

18

tiles, are absent in the turtle, for it has no use for them.

The laminae, covering the interlocking plates of bone, are semi-transparent. They are formed of a hornlike substance comparable to the scales of a snake or lizard (reflecting the reptilian ancestry of turtles), and are divided into distinct sections known as scutes. Some species of land and sea turtles have substituted a thick layer of skin for the laminae. The most prominent representatives of this form in North America are the "soft-shelled" turtles, but the name is misleading. Their surface may seem softer, but beneath it are the same bony plates found in all other turtles.

The dominance of the shell, the way in which it is integrated with the whole body plan, can be seen most clearly during the development of the embryo of a turtle. The shell first appears as a raised area in the back of the embryo. Referred to as the "anlage," it rapidly expands in every direction, flowing outward in a manner reminiscent of thick, flowing molasses, as one writer has noted. Beneath the anlage the ribs form independently; but as the anlage expands, its influence becomes overwhelming. Its development compels the ribs to remain straight, not curving around as do ours. Soon every part of the turtle's embryonic anatomy has come under the direction of the shell. The shape of the turtle is further determined by the fact that the embryo grows more rapidly in a side-to-side direction than in the more conventional up-and-down development evident in most other reptiles. This pattern of growth produces the characteristic low, flattened shape of the turtle. Curiously, the shell is not finished until after the turtle has freed itself from its egg. For this reason, a supply of calcium is vital to insure the completion of the shell of a young chelonian. Soft-shell, an ailment responsible for the death of young turtles in captivity, is caused by a lack of calcium in the diet: the shell remains incomplete, the turtle is vulnerable to internal damage, and the lack proves fatal.

While the shell itself has been a constant in turtle life for over 100 million years, its shape has been changed repeatedly to meet the pressures of diverse environments. The first turtles had a shell both thick and heavy, as they sacrificed speed for armor to deter the sharp teeth of their carnivorous relatives. After the dinosaurus had lost step with a changing world, and became extinct, such a shell proved more of a burden than asset; so descendants of the original turtle line created a number of variations on the basic model. Three different kinds of variations can be seen in species now alive.

When several species of turtles turned back to the sea for refuge and sustenance, they found a very bulky shell to be a severe drawback. Some species jettisoned the horny laminae, replacing them with a smooth layer of tough skin. Others developed modifications of their shells that maintained the laminae while reducing their density. Several kinds of marine turtles now sport an incomplete plastron. To increase their speed in the water, marine turtles substituted flippers for clawed limbs. The placement of the bones connected with the movement of the limbs changed, adding power to the flippers. The sea-going turtles still active, though in diminished numbers, in the world today are capable of attaining the greatest speeds of any living reptile. The Atlantic leatherback turtle is said to be capable of bursts of speed of as much as 100 meters in ten seconds, making it, were it interested, an Olympic contender. More importantly, such bursts of speed can carry it rapidly away from any disturbance or threat. However, in securing speed in the water, the marine turtles have had to sacrifice agility on the land. Their movements, when the females emerge from the ocean to breed, or when both sexes come out to bask in the sun, are slow and labored.

The turtles that have become exclusively land dwellers have also shed much of the thickness of their ancestors' shells. This was necessary to increase their mobility, and to give them the ability to easily enter a variety of small apertures and to manuever through dense cover. Moreover, while reduced in thickness, the shells of some land species have become noticeably elevated, probably as a self-serving defense modification. Some land species, such as the desert tortoise, have made use of the elevated shell to create a space for the storage of additional water. Lacking the speed of their water-dwelling relatives, some tortoises have transverse hinges in their shells. When the animal is threatened and withdraws, the hinges allow the shell to be either partially or completely closed. The most extreme example of adaptation to the land is seen among the soft-shelled tortoises of Africa. According to Carr, this species, living in rocky terrain, has such a reduced carapace that it has become remarkably supple. It can "squeeze itself into narrow rock crevices or beneath or between boulders, inflate its body with air like a toad caught by a snake, and resist the most determined efforts to extricate it." (P. 25.)

The soft-shelled species of North America provide yet another example of evolutionary modifications of the shell. In them, the hard laminae of the carapace have been entirely discarded, in favor of a light, though tough, layer of skin overlaying the bones. In contrast to the land tortoise, with their elevated shells, the softshells have a very flat carapace. The edges of their carapace lack the peripheral bones found in other turtles, making the margins of the shell thin and soft. In addition, softshells have rather long, very flexible necks.

While the need for easy, rapid movement in water has brought about certain modifications of the shell, other factors may have been even more influential in the changes wrought on it. To catch their food, soft-shelled turtles spend most of their time concealed in the oozy mud found on the bottoms of lakes, ponds, or streams, waiting for prey to pass by. On the defensive side, they prefer a location in shallow water, for them the long neck can carry the turtle's head above the surface for respiration without its being compelled to move and give itself away. The flatness of the shell and its color patterns and configurations favor its concealment in bottom deposits. The soft edges of its shell, notes Carr, "conform readily to bottom contours and make it easy for the turtles to shuffle themselves into sand or silt." (P. 26.) So while locomotion played some part in the development of the softshells, their carnivorous diet and their need for a safer habitat probably played a much greater role.

The shell, then, has undergone a number of modifications, proving the turtles to be especially capable of adapting to differing environments and pressures. The sign of a good idea isn't only its insight, but its malleability, the ways in which it lends itself to a number of variations.

In and Around the Shell

To make it possible to withdraw the head within the shell, a special arrangement of neck vertebrae and muscles proved necessary. Indeed, given the largely immovable body of the turtle, the head itself has retained an impressive mobility. Without that mobility, the shell would be of little value, for the vulnerable head would yet be fair game for any predator. Movement of the head, then, is a life-and-death matter. So it makes good sense that the design of the neck is important enough to function as a primary means of classifying turtles.

Side-neck turtles, or Pleurodira, withdraw their heads by bending their necks to one side. Species of Pleurodira once occurred in North America; but, for an unknown reason, all of them became extinct. Today families belonging to the Pleurodira sub-order are found in South America, Africa, and Australia.

All of the turtles found in North America are Cryptodira; that is, turtles that withdraw their heads by folding the neck into an S-shaped curve. The very specialized neck of these turtles has eight vertebrae (mammals have only seven). The muscles of the neck are especially flexible. Likewise, the skin about the neck stretches or retracts with the muscles, allowing the turtle's head freedom of movement.

The skin of the turtle complements and completes the protection of the shell. It is tough, with a leather-like consistency. Its many wrinkles and folds—loosest around the neck—allow for extension and retraction of the head, and for movement of the limbs and tail. (The head is nonetheless protected with a layer of thick, scaly skin, while the tail is sheathed with two layers of hard skin.) If you examine a turtle's skin, you'll find that it has scales, similar to those found on other reptiles.

The scales of all reptiles are often thought of in the same mistaken way as the shell of a turtle—as a suit of armor fitted over the complete, naked form beneath. In fact, however, the turtle's scales, like its shell, are not simply a "covering" for the body, but rather integral with the body itself. Scales *are* skin, modified over the ages to afford reptiles additional protection from the rough demands of varying environments.

On the legs the scales are larger, overlapping, and somewhat tougher than on other portions of the skin. This has evolved because the legs are critical to the survival of the creature; aside from the head, the legs are the only target of any size for predators and are, of course, the turtle's means of locomotion on land and in water. Indeed, the nature of the skin and the highly specialized forms it has taken are crucial to the turtle's limb functions and general locomotive abilities.

The nails of the turtle's foot are modified, hardened extensions of its skin; they grow to varying lengths among different species (although some species have no nails at all). Thick, handy for shredding food and for excavating, the nails are also used for climbing—which some species of turtles do with frequency. The nails dig for leverage while the body pushes forward. Altogether, the turtle's limbs are not only tough, they are quite strong. If a turtle falls onto its back or is upended during a battle with a competitor, it will stretch its forearm over its head and dig its nails into the ground. Using the leg as a lever, it will push itself back over. And carry on.

Locomotion and limb structure among aquatic species naturally have their own specialized characteristics. It has frequently been noted that sea turtles appear to "fly" through the water. The comparison is not inappropriate. The streamlined bodies of marine turtles offer little resistance to the water. They lack toes, and generally lack claws, having instead the broad, unbroken surface of a flipper. The front flippers of a sea turtle are longer than the hind ones. Terrifically powerful, the front flippers—used together—drive downward in vertical strokes much like the movements of a bird's wings. Hind flippers are used mainly to steer the turtle. Fresh-water aquatic turtles, on the other hand, are not so specialized. While their limbs are webbed, they do have distinct clawed toes and are still capable of speed, though not of the great propulsive movements of a sea turtle. Many fresh-water turtles also walk underwater to investigate the life forms gathered around clumps of aquatic plants for possible additions to their diet.

The development and form of its shell, the modifications of its skeleton, the design of its neck, and the features of its skin and locomotor systems all make the turtle a most astonishing creature. Evolving always to meet the demands of changing and frequently hostile environments, the line of turtles experienced a series of remarkable developments, not the least of which was a unique method of respiration.

For a long time observers of turtles were baffled by the method of chelonian respiration. A turtle's shell does not expand and contract, making it impossible for the creature to draw in air in the way favored by mammals. Some early herpetologists theorized that turtles breathed in a manner similar to frogs or toads—that is, by using muscles in their throat to draw air in. But, in fact, three unique muscles not part of the throat mechanism are used to control breathing. Two of these muscles, located in the leg sockets below the vital organs, function to enlarge the body cavity so that air may enter the lungs. A third, complex muscle then comes into action, working to push the organs against the lungs, thus inflating them and forcing air out. This action is audible to us only when we encounter a turtle by surprise: as it withdraws its head and limbs, the air pressed out of its lungs can be heard as a drawn-out hiss. The turtle isn't attempting to sound sinister or threatening; the hissing action is involuntary.

The pulsations in the throat noticed by the original herpetologists and mistaken for the primary means of respiration are actually of secondary importance. Turtles that have adapted to life in fresh and salt water use their mouth cavities as a sort of gill. As water is drawn in through the nasal openings, dissolved oxygen is isolated from it, absorbed within the mouth cavity and the water is then expelled. Soft-shelled turtles can also absorb oxygen through their skins. Some aquatic species can supplement their supply of oxygen by withdrawing it from water drawn into two thin-walled sacs located around the anal opening.

The turtle's entirely original method of respiration provides a much more thorough ventilation of the lungs than we are capable of. Chelonians have not only a relatively low oxygen requirement, but are capable of rather astounding periods of non-respiration. At least one herpetologist has suggested that the turtle's need for oxygen is so modest that some species can survive on as little as one breath every two hours! Archie Carr cites a record of a turtle's survival for twenty-four hours in a container filled with pure nitrogen. It is not impossible for turtles to go for days underwater without experiencing any respiratory difficulty, drawing their necessary oxygen through the anal opening or mouth cavity. Unique methods of respiration, then, combined with a limited need for oxygen, give the turtle a further degree of freedom from persecution. If disturbed, the turtle can withdraw into itself and remain withdrawn—until even the most patient of predators will despair.

Perception and Intelligence

Development and structure of the turtle's body, we have seen, shows some remarkable features, most of which are readily comprehensible in terms of basic survival and environmental adaptation. As for the creature's mental and sensorial modes, however, the picture is not so clear. The turtle's sense of hearing, for example, is not well understood. Whereas the chelonian ear *is* well-developed, and should thus be capable of rather acute sound reception, experiments conducted over the past thirty years have been unable to discover *any* evidence of keen hearing. Instead, some researchers have found that turtles have developed an almost preternatural ability to "hear" vibrations—even vibrations emanating from quite a distance that are quite faint to human ears. And turtles can be quite discriminating in judging the distance and degree of danger signaled by a vibration.

The chelonian voice, like much else having to do with turtles' communicative modes, remains a controversial subject. Many instances of a turtle's *apparent vocalization* are now thought to be caused by sounds attending the exhalation of breath, the grinding together of jaws, or the frictional contact between body parts. Sea turtles, however, can both roar and grunt. And the giant male tortoises of the Galapagos Islands are known to roar during intercourse. Indeed, all instances of chelonian vocalization so far recorded seem to occur in connection with mating. Belief in the ability of turtles to "talk" appears to have been nearly universal, occurring again and again in the tales of very divergent cultures. *Spargis*, the term used for many years to denote the sea-going leatherback turtle, derives from the Greek word for "to make a noise." Yet the ability of turtles to emit regular, intentional patterns of sound is apparently very limited. To be sure, vocalization is a subject needing further field study.

Few experiments have been carried out to determine the degree of sensitivity of the turtle's sense of smell. Those that have been done suggest that the olfactory sense is acute. The pulsations so noticeable in the necks of turtles are thought to be connected in some way with their ability to smell. Very specific odors, especially those of some foodstuffs, elicit the strongest response from turtles. The sense of taste also seems to be well developed: a turtle will take a substance into its mouth and, finding it in some way objectionable, spit it out—such a mannerism likely indicating an objection to taste.

The turtle further undermines its image as a stolid, unfeeling creature by its very well-developed sense of touch. Its ability to judge articles by touch is both sure and sensitive, as demonstrated in the great gentleness and assured manner with which a female can, using only a hind foot, arrange the eggs in her just-excavated nest. Given the inability of most turtles to maneuver quickly or with any degree of suppleness, it is easy to understand how the sense of touch can become all-important. When a turtle has neither the time nor the suppleness to turn quickly to *observe* a situation, the sense of touch must tell everything.

Eyesight among turtles is evidently quite keen. Most species can distinguish red, yellow, green, blue, and violet; their total range of color perception approaches our own, although it is unlikely that they can see objects clearly at great distance, or pick out objects at mid-distances with as much clarity as humans. Turtles having vivid colorings on their shells tend to respond more quickly to colors at the red end of the spectrum than to other colors, possibly because these are the colors most commonly occurring on chelonian shells. In experiments testing their ability to discriminate visually, several species of turtles learned to distinguish between lines of varying widths, recognizing a difference in line thickness of as little as one millimeter. Old age or illness can cause blindness in turtles; in their natural surroundings such an affliction must frequently prove fatal.

The degree of turtle intelligence forms a much misunderstood and hotly disputed subject. Compared to man, turtles would seem to be decidedly dim creatures. So, of course, would almost all animals, excepting porpoises, wolves, and some few others. Compared to turtles, however, men have many woeful shortcomings. Our sense of direction is not nearly so good. Our ability to travel underwater without artificial contrivances is much more severely limited. We're no good at all at holding our breath. And it is much less likely that our individual lifespans will ever match the turtle's characteristic longevity.

The point, of course, is that *using our own braininess as a measuring stick for other forms of life is not only misleading, but chauvinistic.* On the fallacy of viewing animals in terms of the progress of human evolution, naturalist writer Henry Beston has this to say in *The Outermost House*:

> We need another and a wiser and perhaps a more mystical concept of animals. Remote from universal nature, and living by complicated artifice, man in civilization surveys the creature through the glass of his knowledge and sees thereby a feather magnified and the whole image in distortion. We patronize them for their incompleteness, for their tragic fate of having taken form so far below ourselves. And therein we err, and greatly err. For the animal shall not be measured by man. In a world older and more complete than ours they move finished and complete, gifted with extensions of the sense we have lost or never attained, living by voices we shall never hear. They are not brethren, they are not un-

derlings; they are other nations, caught with ourselves in the net of life and time, fellow prisoners of the splendour and travail of the earth. [Pp. 19-20.]

Indeed, turtles have faced conditions very different from those which our ancestors encountered, and have responded to those conditions in the manner dictated by their form and needs. Turtles haven't, generally, failed at anything they've attempted. It is more accurate, and realistic, to view them as eminently successful reptiles who have found their way in the world and stuck to it. "Slow and steady wins the race" is a lesson that pertains to evolution as well as fable.

While their physical progress—though persistent—is justly regarded as laborious and slow, their ability to learn quickly and perform well in such tasks as running mazes has been noted. Yet herpetologists studying turtles have generally restricted themselves to experiments in which the qualities of personality and intelligence have been depreciated or ignored. In the rather skimpy literature on the experiences of the keepers and the kept, we do find *some* indications of chelonian intelligence. The unfortunate scarcity of this literature suggests that few people have thought it worthwhile either to set down or publish such materials.

I have gained my own admitted admiration for turtle intelligence from a number of conversations with private collectors of turtles—people quite willing to share their experiences, but who have rarely been asked. I have heard repeatedly of the shrewd ability of turtles to quickly identify the person responsible for bringing them food and to watch closely for signs of feeding behavior. One turtle, who typically approached its owner after the latter was seated for dinner, cast what seemed to be imploring looks toward the food. Another waited by the refrigerator. When its keeper approached, it would expect food, having identified the refrigerator as the source of meals. If food was not forthcoming, the turtle would climb up onto its owner's foot to make certain that it was not being overlooked. Turtles in zoos are said to become quite familiar, not only with their keepers, but with those times of day when they are to be fed. One finds again and again, if one looks in the right places, considerable evidence of very distinct personalities and varying degrees of intelligence among turtles.

The sourcebooks seem to agree that terrestrial and fresh-water species are more intelligent than salt-water species. However, I would tend to discount this conclusion, since so little is still known of the lives and activities of sea-going chelonians. The great part of their lives is carried on out of the sight of men, and their capabilities (aside from their well-known and outstanding ability at navigation) have not been tested.

Turtles in captivity, on the other hand, reveal a bit more of themselves. Curiously, when kept captive in groups rather than in individual enclosures, turtles tend to work out an elementary hierarchy, with deference independently paid to certain members of the group. And though turtles often do pursue a solitary life, their tendency to social grouping is, I think, quite interesting. Such activity reflects either the remnant of a once necessary behavior pattern (since outmoded) or—more likely—an intelligent response to a potentially antagonistic situation.

No final statement can be made on the braininess of turtles; nor should one be necessary. It is sufficient to say that turtles embody mind-power enough to have adapted and survived in a variety of challenging situations. Yet it would be quite humanly short-sighted not to remark that turtles have achieved their enduring form without wreaking havoc on other species or polluting their environment. They have found, following their own bodies, their place in the world—a world that is, finally, as much theirs as our own.

2

Courtship, Mating, and Reproduction

The manner in which turtles reproduce their kind is a mystery to most of us. Few know how it is accomplished, and fewer still have observed firsthand such chelonian intimacies. Indeed, even among those who have studied reproductive behavior in turtles there are yet many questions that remain unanswered. The age at which different turtles achieve sexual maturity, for instance, seems to vary not only between species, but even among members of a particular species.

While most species of North American turtles are sexually mature by about four years of age, this is only an average, and there may be variations from one species to the next. Information on just how long it takes for a turtle to reach its full growth is scarce. Box turtles, one study suggests, take about twenty years. Barring accidents, box turtles can go on to live another fifty years. The largest turtle is the leatherback, a marine species which regularly attains a weight of 1500 pounds, and in some instances may even reach a ton. (The Galapagos tortoises, by comparison, have an upper weight limit of about 570 pounds.) The largest North American species is the alligator snapper, with the heavyweight crown going to a specimen slightly over 400 pounds.

Such figures are, indeed, spectacular; but they don't answer the essential questions—how long does it take for a turtle to reach sexual maturity, and how many years are required for a turtle to complete its growth? Surprisingly, there are as many questions surrounding the familiar turtle as the most shadowy and uncommon of creatures. But here we will focus on what *is* known, starting with the structure that makes it all possible.

At first glance, the shell of the turtle would seem to present an insurmountable problem to any sex life at all. It doesn't, of course. But, like in all aspects of turtle life, the way in which turtles mate and reproduce has been largely determined by the structure and overriding influence of the shell.

The simplest way of identifying the sex of a turtle is by examining its tail. The tail of the male is longer, and broader, than the female's. The male's anus is located farther away from the body, along the tail, than the female's. Also located in the tail is the penis of the male. Usually lying out of sight, it is extruded through the anus during copulation. The male must therefore have a long tail to allow the penis to be brought into contact with the sexual organs of the female, which are located at the base of the tail. For copulation, the tail of the male is curled down and around as the male mounts the female from behind. This particular arrangement of the reproductive organs was necessitated by the presence of the shell: to have retained the sexual organs in the trunk of the turtle would have required a breach in the shell, which in turn would have made the turtle more vulnerable. Another anatomical adaptation to facilitate reproduction occurs in some species in which the males have a slightly concave plastron to better accept the convex carapace of the female, enabling the male to move in yet more closely. Actually, the whole arrangement is rather convenient for turtles, as the long history of their form would suggest. Had copulation been so difficult as to be a discouragement, turtles would have disappeared long ago.

The Sex Life of Fresh-Water and Land Turtles

Fresh-water aquatic turtles mate in the water. Terrestrial species mate either on land or in water. (Marine, or sea-going, turtles are discussed in the last section of this chapter.) Courtship procedures vary greatly from species to species. In some, the male simply pursues the female and unceremoniously mounts her. Other species show more elaborate behavior, during which the male bites the neck or shell of the female, or pushes her rather roughly about before mounting her.

Perhaps the most touching behavior belongs to the males of the North American painted turtles and to the males of the yellow-bellied, red-eared, Cumberland, Rio Grande, and Baja California subspecies. In all of them the male swims backward before the female while stroking or lightly tapping her face with the greatly elongated fingernails common to the males. At another extreme, the courtship behavior of a few species of North American tortoises tends to be rather rough. The male rams the shell of the female and frequently gives her repeated bites.

Snapping turtles have been observed to perform a sort of sinuous courtship dance in which a male and female face each other and make "sudden, simultaneous sideward sweeps of their heads and necks, but in opposite directions; subsequently they slowly brought their necks back to the straight-forward position" (Ernst and Barbour, p. 22).

Box turtles sustain a rather lengthy courtship procedure. A male will approach a female, stop about four inches away, and assume a pose—head erect, legs straight, sometimes with one leg raised above the ground. He will then circle the female, nudging her, even giving her a hard push, and biting her shell. The three-toed box turtle somewhat alters this behavior. Instead of walking around the female, the male will pause before her and pulsate his bright orange-colored throat. This is apparently sufficiently convincing to the female, for soon afterwards the male will mount her. On a more somber note, it has been observed that after intercourse males of the species sometimes fall onto their backs in terrain where they cannot get enough leverage to turn themselves over. When they cannot right themselves, the turtles die.

Wood turtles, like snappers, have been observed to engage in a sort of courtship dance. Male and female approach each other and, when they are facing each other at a distance of a little more than half a foot, begin to swing their heads rhythmically from side to side. This ritual may go on for as long as two hours without pause. One field observation included a report of wood turtles whistling during courtship; they produced a thin, high-pitched sound resembling the whistle of a teapot.

While male wood turtles often initiate the action, females have been observed in a strongly aggressive role. With the painted turtle, on the other hand, the action is generally very mild. Males seek out females, and use their foreclaws to stroke the female's head and neck. An interested female will respond by using her foreclaws to stroke his outstretched limbs.

Much more dynamic, the male spotted turtle engages in wild pursuit of the female. Sometimes a female may be chased by more than one male. In such circumstances the males may stop the pursuit to fight one another until a victor emerges. Losers give up and retreat.

The male stinkpot, named for the odious aroma of its muck glands, which it voids when threatened, is also a rather aggressive swain. Having identified a female by the feeling of her tail, or by smelling some distinctly feminine aroma, the male will pursue her on land or in water, nudging her repeatedly. If she consents, he will mount her while continuing to nudge and rub her about the head.

River cooters have been seen to perform a close, slow dance under water as a preliminary to mating. Their common name—cooter—though its history is somewhat confusing, apparently has built-in reference to the turtle's sexuality. Some three hundred years ago, "cooting" was the term used by English narrators to describe the intercourse of chelonians. (There is some evidence to suggest that the word was derived from a term used by slaves taken from West Africa, and is thus originally an African word for turtle or water turtle.)

Striped mud turtles have shown some remarkable courtship behavior. An incident observed by Archie Carr and summarized by Ernst and Barbour reminds us of the behavioral variability within a species and, simultaneously, of our still incomplete understanding of courtship activities. Carr observed two males of the striped mud species fighting on the bank of a stream. A female of the species was several feet away. One of the males was shoved off balance and fell into the water. The victor then went to the female, "thrust his snout beneath her plastron, and crawled under her, leaving her balanced upon his carapace" (Ernst and Barbour, p. 57). They retained this unusual position for a half hour.

As pointed out earlier, during matings the males of the giant land tortoises of the Galapagos Islands roar, at roughly five-second intervals. Indeed, this is thought to be the only time when the tortoises emit any sound. It is not known whether any species of North American turtles can or do emit sounds during copulation. I have seen photographs showing both male and female with necks greatly extended, and with the female's jaws agape: though it would be difficult to prove, their poses do indicate a very real excitement, a feeling of profound pleasure. As my suspicions could not be *disproved*, I prefer to think of chelonian intimacy as something more than mere necessity for the continuance of species.

The Nest, the Egg, and the Hatchling

In China, alongside the veneration of the turtle as a symbol of longevity, there seems to have existed a tradition of regarding the turtle as a fickle lover and an inconstant parent. To call someone a "turtle" might thus be interpreted as a distinct insult. While it is true that they resume their individual concerns after copulation, and that the female's concern for her egg ends with the camouflage of her nest, turtles are not alone in such behavior. And a rationale for the pattern, though not always discernible, is undoubtedly there. With all the information they need to survive already encoded in body and brain, new hatchlings emerge from their eggs. A mother's presence, while it would be helpful, is not vital; it may be that infant turtles are more successful at surviving by separating and following their own individual, secretive paths. In the case of sea turtles, whose babies emerge by the score from a nest, any sort of parental behavior would be ineffectual—even if the female were capable of identifying her own brood.

Mating occurs with increasing frequency during the spring and reaches a peak by early summer. The sperm of the male can be retained in the genital tract of the female for as long as four years, continuing to fertilize eggs. However, the percentage of fertile eggs in clutches laid after the first season declines each succeeding year. A single mating is sufficient to fertilize the eggs the female has produced. Most of the year's eggs will have been laid by mid-July. In the northern areas of the continent the eggs *must* be laid by then to allow sufficient time for incubation and for the emergence of the hatchlings at least several weeks before the onset of cold weather. In some cases, very advanced embryos or just-hatched babies remain nested below ground in a state of hibernation throughout the winter, delaying their emergence until spring.

After mating, the females of every species seek out the right location to excavate a nest. The nest may be dug in sand, soil, or a decaying mound of leaf mold and other organic matter. Every species digs the same sort of nest: a flask-shaped hole which is as deep as the length of the fully extended hind leg. To make the ground softer and easier to excavate, several kinds of turtles wet the soil with water stored in their bladder. In some species the female uses her feet to arrange the eggs as they are laid, and gently tamps loose soil around them. After all the eggs have been dropped in place, the hind feet push soil into the nest until the hole has been filled in. The female then uses one of a variety of methods to camouflage or disguise the site. She might scuffle the surface of the nest to eradicate any trace of activity; or pound the spot flat with her plastron; or fling sand or soil about the area so that several locations seem to be indicated. Some species crawl back and forth over the nesting area, creating a general impression of disturbance without indicating the specific site. After her labors, the female's task is done, and she departs the site.

Most species of turtles produce rather small, elliptical eggs. The eggs are white, in contrast to the eggs of such distant relatives as the birds. While many birds' eggs are pigmented, having a mottled surface, to disguise them from predators, turtle eggs are incubated beneath the ground and pigmentation therefore has no value. Predators with a taste for turtle eggs search them out by smell or by some other more subtle sense.

The reptilian egg, developed by the cotylosaurs (stem reptiles), is a much more complex piece of work than it appears. Because the embryo is not attached to the mother, it must contain within itself all the nourishment the developing turtle will need. Like in the hen's egg, the yolk is the reserve of nourishment and the white is the water reserve. In the turtle there is a much larger percentage of yolk than white: to gain increased nutrients, water was sacrificed. A hen's egg is by weight about 11% shell, 56% white (water), and 33% yolk. By contrast, a sea-turtle egg is by weight about 5% shell, 40% white, and 55% yolk. As these figures might suggest, the shell of the turtle egg is sufficiently permeable to allow additional moisture to reach the embryo. Various gases necessary for proper embryonic development also pass through the permeable surface of the chelonian eggshell.

Every embryo gives off waste products as it develops. If not promptly removed, these wastes would rapidly destroy the embryo. In fish, amphibians, and mammals the wastes are rendered into soluble urea. In mammals, this toxic waste product is dissolved and carried away through the mother's bloodstream; among fish and amphibians, the urea is dissolved and dissipated as soon as it is generated. Turtles have developed an alternative method of handling the problem. The wastes are transformed into insoluble uric acid, which cannot penetrate the embryo, and are stored within the egg in the space between the embryo and the eggshell. As in all other matters, turtles have here added their own unique developments to basic principles. And the turtle egg has existed, in unchanged form, for 100 million years.

When a baby turtle first emerges from its egg, it sports a projection on its mouth referred to as an "egg tooth." (Turtles lack teeth, having instead jaws equipped with either sharp horny ridges or a broad crushing surface, powerful enough to shred or mash all but the toughest of foodstuffs.) When a turtle is ready to emerge from its egg, it uses the egg tooth to pierce a hole in the egg and then to diligently pick away until the hole is sufficiently large for the baby to crawl through. The egg tooth, really a temporary extension of the upper jaw, will disappear as the turtle grows.

The larger the turtle, the more eggs she will lay. Sea turtles lay the largest number of eggs at a time, both because of their size and because of the pressure put on them by predators. The egg-laying record for a North American species seems to be held by a snapping turtle in Canada who laid eighty eggs in one nest. Larger clutches may certainly be possible, though they are rare. While most North American turtles lay only one clutch a year, some species may produce as many as three nests; but the evidence on this subject is incomplete. We know no average number of eggs for a species. Indeed, little evidence yet exists from which to draw any general rules or averages. This is not because sufficient nests have not been dug up by humans; rather, the people generally doing the digging haven't been doing it for science, but for their stomachs. And although humans have had some success at discovering turtle eggs, non-human predators have a good deal more. The eggs of the sea turtle are most often in danger; yet every species of turtle on the continent suffers from raids. Only by producing clutches every year can turtles maintain their numbers. Now, as the areas in which they naturally dig their nests are diminishing, some kinds of turtles retain only the most precarious hold on existence.

The period of incubation—subject to great variation due to environmental conditions—is generally from two to three months. When the turtles do emerge from their eggs, they tend to do so at about the same time throughout a clutch. This occurs because the eggs have all received the same degree of warmth and developed at about the same rate. Moreover, group emergence acts to preserve at least some of the hatchlings in each batch. As they emerge, solitary arrivals could easily and quickly be picked off by predators—but a group presents a more confusing prospect: with baby turtles moving in a number of directions (or, as with sea turtles, moving in one direction in a great stampede), at least a few of the defenseless hatchlings should survive because of the confusion of the moment.

After they emerge, hatchlings soon disappear. Their vanishing is so nearly complete that almost no substantiated facts exist to create an image of their first year of life. Wariness, the excellent camouflage of their generally dull bodies, and the ability to exist for some time without much food all contribute to their success away. By the time a turtle reappears, its soft shell has hardened into armor, making the animal relatively safe from predation.

The disappearance of the fledgling turtles soon after they emerge from their eggs, and their absence until maturity, may be more than a technique for survival. It may also indicate very distinct dietary differences between adults and their young. Almost every record of turtle life compiled over a lengthy time span mentions the lack of infant or adolescent turtles in an area well populated with adults. In the case of the wood turtle, this absence is largely explainable by the infant's definite preference for meat (in the form of worms and other small creatures active in bodies of fresh water). Adults, on the other hand, are vegetarians. The immature wood turtles spend their early years in habitats where the palate may be satisfied—in the marshy borders of ponds, streams, and lakes. As they mature, their tastes in food undergo a slow change, bringing them out of the water and drawing them farther and farther afield.

Now, such behavior does have survival value. During their most vulnerable period, turtles are hidden away in thick grasses on oozy ground, a location not much frequented by predators capable of killing baby turtles. It is an intriguing possibility, then, that changes in diet may account for the disappearance of other chelonian youngsters besides the wood turtle. When we search for young turtles in the locations habitually occupied by adults, we may simply be looking in the wrong place.

The Loves of the Sea Turtle

The courtship and mating behavior of sea turtles, while basically similar to that of land or fresh-water turtles, differs somewhat because of the more challenging environment of the oceans. The nesting behavior of sea turtles is quite distinctive, involving special challenges that other species do not face. Audubon, the artist responsible for the first accurate paintings of American wildlife, noted in his journals that "the loves of the sea turtle are conducted in a most extraordinary manner . . ." And so they are.

Sea turtles mate either below or on the surface of the water, the below-surface position being the more common. The males of some species engage in a delicate ballet display before mounting a female. How long copulation lasts is unknown. It is possible among some species that the union could last for hours. As in all matters, turtles are generally unhurried.

Representatives of each of the marine species of turtles browse the rich coastal waters of the continent. But only two species still come ashore to excavate nests and lay eggs on the beaches of North America. The Atlantic loggerhead and the Atlantic ridley, differing in small ways from the Pacific versions of their species, dig nests along stretches of the southern coastline. Two other marine species, the Atlantic green turtle and the hawksbill, once also laid their eggs along the southern coasts. However, the green and the hawksbill had the misfortune of having, respectively, tender flesh and a valuable shell. In addition, their eggs were easily gathered because these species tended to come together off certain beaches. The loggerhead and ridley, by contrast, come ashore individually or in small numbers along widely scattered stretches of coastline, making it impossible to gather very many females or eggs, or to depend on their annual appearance in the same spot.

The green and hawksbill females and their eggs had been under pressure for several hundred years, beginning with the Indians along the Florida coast and continuing, more emphatically, after the appearance of white men. By the end of the nineteenth century, those groups of green and hawksbill turtles that had returned to Florida for generation after generation to nest had become all but extinct. It appears to have been their particular weakness to have handed down, through imprinting at birth or through some genetic code, the direction for each succeeding generation to return to the same area, even the same beach, where they emerged from their eggs. This phenomenon is still apparent in the scant remnants of the Atlantic green turtle who return, in greatly diminished numbers, to certain beaches of Central America to lay their eggs. At one time, as recently as three hundred years ago, different groups of green turtles had breeding sites in Florida, the West Indies, Vera Cruz, and on Ascension Island. There has been no verified report of a green turtle nest in Florida for over forty years.

The manner in which a nest is excavated and eggs are laid differs somewhat from species to species, but not so greatly that a description of the loggerhead's method of reproduction cannot serve as a summary for all. The effort of the female marine turtle is heroic enough to deserve more than passing mention, even though our primary concern is with species indigenous to North America. (Drawing the line between ocean and land mass is something that herpetologists, like politicians, are often hard put to do.)

The loggerhead is the least tropical of all marine turtles in its choices of nesting grounds. Most species come ashore to lay eggs only in latitudes below North America. The green, hawksbill, and ridley nested no farther north than Florida. But the loggerheads have been known to lay eggs as far north as the Virginia coast, and still regularly nest along the coastline from Georgia to Florida. This is not entirely surprising, for the loggerhead is also the most daring of marine turtles when it comes to exploring the fringes of the North American continent. Loggerheads have been regularly observed in coastal bays; they are known to enter coastal streams in marsh areas and ascend them until further progress is stopped by a greatly narrowed passage or by a loss of the water's salinity due to mingling with fresh water from the interior. It is possible, but not proven, that loggerheads have made ascensions of the Mississippi river. The great range that loggerheads cover, and their willingness to explore areas most other marine turtles shun, would seem to indicate a hardy and adaptable creature.

Like all marine turtles, male and female loggerheads are drawn by some unknown interior compass to meet in the area just beyond the surf of certain beaches. As loggerheads are solitary travelers throughout their lives, just how numbers of them are at the same time drawn to meet in the same location—out of the entire coastline stretching between Virginia and Florida—is a mystery. Females come ashore and wait for the evening before emerging. Though beaches open to the sea are preferred, a primary consideration seems to be the looseness of the sand. A beach having a hard, compacted surface is generally not used.

The females may emerge anytime from April to August, with the greatest frequency seeming to be in June. Hauling along their bulky bodies by means of flippers, the turtles make their tedious journey to a point located somewhere between the high tide mark and the dunes. It is not uncommon for loggerheads to come ashore, dig a few test holes, and return to the sea, delaying the business of egg-laying until some subtle element, unknown to us, is present.

Throughout the excavating process the female utters audible gasps. And from the moment she emerges from the ocean until she returns, the female weeps large, briny tears. Although many different cultures have attributed these tears to the mother's helpless realization of the quick death that will overtake most of her offspring, the tears are actually necessary to keep the eyes moist and free of sand.

The nest is excavated with the remarkably dextrous hind flippers. These specialized modifications of the reptilian limb are capable of shoveling up a load of sand, holding it in place by curling back their margins to form a cup, and then straightening out and flinging the load aside. The hind flippers withdraw sand to the greatest depth they can reach, generally one-and-a-half to just over two feet, and to a width of ten inches. Then the female thrusts her tail into the hole, extends her ovipositor (specialized egg-laying organ) from the anal opening, and begins to drop eggs into the hole, singly or doubly, at the rate of six to twelve per minute. During the egg-laying process, the turtle cannot be shaken from its activity. Even a noisy group of onlookers crowding closely about will not cause it to cease. (Some observers, showing more curiosity than sense, have even stooped behind the female to catch the falling eggs.) After the eggs have been laid, a total ranging from 120 to 150, the female fills in the nest by gently brushing sand in with her hind flippers. She will pause at intervals to use the flippers to press the sand down. When the hole has been filled in, the loggerhead will pound the site down with her plastron. Using all four flippers, she will fling sand about the area to further disguise the location of the nest. Such efforts do hide the location from men; but rats, skunks, raccoons, and bears seem to have little trouble in turning up the eggs. In Central America, coyotes and jaguars have in the past been observed to appear in numbers on nesting beaches, searching for eggs. How do they know when to turn up?

Females may lay eggs as often as three times in a year. And this is not excessive. Although no average estimate is possible, it has been suggested that the fertility of marine turtle eggs is sometimes as low as fifty percent. Many predators regularly take the eggs. But the most devastating blow falls after the turtles hatch. The time required for hatching varies greatly, depending on the conditions of the environment. Archie Carr cites periods of from 31 to 65 days, indicating the wide variation. When the time arrives, the young loggerheads come out together, first emerging from their shells and then, after a rest of several hours, breaking into the open. With only the slightest hesitation, they unerringly head for the ocean. According to Carr, "the cues which direct the hatchlings toward the sea have been found experimentally to include a tendency toward downhill locomotion (once the nest has been left behind) and an inclination toward the level sea horizon and away from the broken shore horizon" (p. 391).

Their brief journey is a perilous one. Gulls, ospreys, and hawks often flock together during such an emergence, swooping down to pluck the struggling infants (whose shells are yet soft) from the sand. The majority of hatchlings often don't survive their first day. And once in the water the threat does not abate. Other predators are waiting to strike into the greatly diminished and defenseless group. Frequently, only a few infants out of a brood of over a hundred make it out to sea. Once in the water, the hatchlings disappear; survivors are rarely spotted again until they are several years old.

The marine species have good reasons for being the most prolific of all turtles: without such large and frequent egg production, they could never have survived the pressures of predation.

3

Habitat and Behavior

In the two preceding chapters, we have been discussing various aspects of chelonian life without referring much to the environment. This has been done to more clearly render certain topics. Having done that, it is important now to place turtles within their natural context, to show in greater detail how turtles have met the challenges of existence across a wide variety of environments. These environments fall rather clearly into several major categories: oceans, marshlands, bodies of fresh water (such as rivers, streams, and ponds), and terrestrial habitats, including woodlands, deserts, and prairies. If you go seeking turtles, you must look in such environments for them.

It is the intention of this chapter to illustrate the various ways in which turtles have adapted to environments in North America, and to point out some of the ways in which turtles have become integral parts of those environments. A far bulkier work than this would be required to thoroughly cover each of the species and subspecies of North American chelonians. The works of Clifford Pope, Archie Carr, and Carl Ernst and Roger Barbour, cited in the Introduction and Bibliography, each carry out the task with admirable efficiency, with staggering industry, and with great thoroughness. My intent has been to choose the most representative or most interesting species (in some cases, admittedly, a subjective judgment). By these I shall illustrate the basic adaptations which turtles have made to a variety of environments, and explain how they operate within such environments. It is, more particularly, my hope that this chapter will provide sufficient impetus to get the reader outside, looking for turtles, observing them in those environments where they are at home, following their activities as they go about the actions necessary to maintain life. The only way to know a wild creature truly—to have an accurate perception of the complexity of its life and the skills by which it survives—is to understand something of the structure and pressures of an environment, and to follow the animal's behavior *in the wild*. This is not always easy to do. In the case of sea-going chelonians, the obstacle to human study of them is the environment itself.

The Oceans

Large areas of the life history of turtles remain mysteries to us, and nowhere is this more evident than in the natural history of sea turtles. We know comparatively little about their movements, about their development from infancy to maturity, and even about their feeding habits. The source of their navigational abilities, which are among the most remarkable in all the populous animal world, remains unidentified. Their environment has effectively served to frustrate our curiosity, although it has not protected the turtles from exploitation. We can only study them, or kill them, when they come into the shallow waters off the coasts, to feed and to mate, and when the females haul themselves onto beaches to dig nests and lay their eggs. We may still lack much knowledge of marine turtles, but we have learned all we need to know to hunt and kill them, and to find their eggs.

Sea turtles have become so entirely adapted to their environment that it is impossible to think of them outside of it. And it is hard to imagine what their ancestors—those first generations to leave the land and return to the sea—must have looked like, so totally have they altered over the millions of years they have inhabited the seas. Only the land tortoises of the Galapagos and Aldabran Islands generally approach the size of the six species of marine turtles. The leatherback turtle, *Dermochelys coriacea*, is the largest sea turtle, and thus the largest living species of turtle. Adults may achieve a length of up to eight feet and a weight approaching one ton. Such size would be impossible for a turtle in a terrestrial environment: the creature would soon exhaust itself attempting to move about, and would be terrifically vulnerable to attack. Thus the sea has allowed, and may have encouraged, the development of hefty bodies in her chelonian inhabitants.

Life in the seas has also mandated the evolution of the limbs into flippers. These specialized, paddle-shaped movers are marvelously efficient in the water, but of little use on land. Only female sea turtles come ashore, and they emerge only to dig a nest and lay eggs. They have a hard time of it. Their struggle to haul themselves up the gentle incline of a beach is a hard and long one. Using their flippers to gain leverage, they must push themselves forward by main force. It is not surprising that some females have been discovered on nesting beaches wedged in the roots of dead trees, or caught by other obstructions, and lacking the energy or the ability to maneuver around them. However, once they are back in the water, the females are revived, capable of simply floating, buoyed by the water, until they regain their strength. In their chosen element of salt water, sea turtles are capable of quick, delicate maneuvers, and bursts of great speed, as well as the strength to maintain a very steady, sustained pace.

Sea turtles have also carried to its furthest point the chelonian ability to conserve oxygen. Studies indicate that the green turtle has the ability to remain submerged for as long as five hours, sustaining itself on a minimal amount of oxygen. Though I am aware of no documentation of such an ability in other species of marine turtles, it would seem likely that such an adaptation would be found in all of them. Similarly, green turtles have glands that collect and excrete excessive amounts of salt from their blood. A build-up of salt in the blood could prove fatal, so it must again be assumed that other species of sea turtles have a similar arrangement. In a saline environment the need for some protection from absorbing too much salt is vital.

While marine turtles make long journeys out across the vast oceans, many species come fairly close to shore to feed. They have to. The foods they prefer are most abundant near the shoreline. That portion of the oceans directly off the coasts, and beyond the dominance of the waves, has a particularly rich association of plants and animals, including mollusks, mussels, and many species of fish. The ceaseless action of the waves, grinding down the shoreline, returns grounded nutrients to the sea. In addition, rivers and streams flowing into the sea carry more nutrients with them. This great concentration of nutrients is both necessary and responsible for the proliferation of sea plants in this area. The plants, in turn, provide either shelter or food for a great number of life forms, and these forms then supply food for predators. Marine turtles, depending on the species, eat either the plants or the life forms associated with them. Life close to shore is not only very abundant, it is also quite concentrated and relatively easy to find.

The green turtle, *Chelonia mydas,* is the most valuable reptile in the world; yet, as Archie Carr has noted, "it would be difficult to name any animal, comparable at once in economic importance and in the depletion in numbers that it has suffered, that is so poorly known" (p. 349). It has a broad, heart-shaped carapace, ranging from dark olive to brown in color, and frequently having linear patterns of a lighter shade distributed unevenly across its back. Its large scales are separated by thick yellow margins. The skin is usually dark, ranging from brown to black in different individuals. Although the turtle may be distinctly olive in appearance, its common name was derived from its layers of green fat. The Atlantic green turtle appears as far north as New England, as far south as Argentina. It seems most at home in the Caribbean, although it was once abundant off the southern coast of North America. The Pacific green turtle appears occasionally as far north as British Columbia, as far south as Chile. Both subspecies of green turtle also occur in other portions of the world, ranging throughout the Atlantic, Pacific, and Indian Oceans.

The mouth and jaws of the green turtle are well adapted to a diet composed largely of sea grasses. The roof of the turtle's mouth has a series of raised ridges that are capable of gathering and straining clumps of grass. The lower jaw has a strongly serrated edge, useful in sawing and tearing the grasses that grow in dense beds. However, the green turtle is not strictly herbivorous. It has also been reported to take crustaceans, jellyfish, and sponges. In captivity it will accept meat. Juveniles are much more carnivorous than adults, although the reason for this is not clear. Yet the design of the mouth would seem to indicate that, as the turtle matures, there is a definite, though slow, movement away from an exclusively meat diet toward a predominantly herbivorous one.

By contrast, the hawksbill turtle, *Eretmochelys imbricata*, is omnivorous, with a preference for marine invertebrates, such as crustaceans, mollusks, sea urchins, sponges, coral, and the Portuguese man-of-war. Some plants are also consumed. Quite opposite from the green turtle, young hawksbills are thought to be herbivorous, switching to a diet of invertebrates only as they mature. The Portuguese man-of-war, a form of jellyfish having particularly poisonous tendrils, can pose a threat to swimmers; so the hawksbill's consumption of the creature is of some small benefit to man. When chewing its way through a man-of-war, a hawksbill will squeeze its eyes shut, thus protecting the one part of its anatomy vulnerable to the poison of its victim.

The hawksbill gains its common name from its long, narrow snout. You might imagine this feature of its face to resemble a hawk's sharp beak. The carapace is heart-shaped, or, as some commentators have observed, "shield-shaped" (evidently having in mind the shields associated with medieval knights, tapering to a point on the bottom). The rear margin of the carapace has a serrated edge. The carapace is dark brown, possibly with an admixture of dark green. Above this somber layer of its shell is the feature that has so threatened the hawksbill: its transparent and quite beautiful scutes, shot through with pods and "rays of reddish, yellow, fawn color, black or white, or even green" (Carr, p. 368). The full brilliance of these scutes can be observed only after they have been peeled from the turtle. Known, incorrectly, as tortoiseshell, these scutes have been a prized item for centuries. The skin of the limbs and neck is black or dark brown with light-colored margins. The skin of the chin and throat is yellow.

As with the green turtle, there are two subspecies of hawksbill. The Atlantic hawksbill occurs from Brazil north to Massachusetts. The Pacific hawksbill occurs in the warmer portions of the Pacific Ocean, and in the Indian Ocean. It may occasionally come as far north as southern tip of California, and it certainly appears in Baja California; it travels as far south as Peru. Throughout its range, the hawksbill prefers "shallow coastal waters, such as mangrove-bordered bays, estuaries, and lagoons with mud bottoms and little or no vegetation, and in small narrow creeks and passes" (Ernst and Barbour, p. 223). It often enters the preferred habitat of the green turtle, those coastal areas having thick underwater vegetation, and there the two species mingle peacefully. Because its diet differs from that of the green, the hawksbill can afford to be much less particular in its sites. Even where dense vegetation is lacking, the areas close to the shore support a variety of life forms. Not much is known of its behavior, although it is assumed to be active during the daylight hours.

The loggerhead turtle, *Caretta caretta*, is a great wanderer, even for sea turtles. It has been discovered out in the open ocean, as much as 500 miles from the nearest land, plowing along unconcernedly at an even pace. The loggerhead is one of the largest of the marine turtles, with the maximum size reported around nine feet long and about 1000 pounds. The average seems to be slightly in excess of three feet and weighs 300 pounds. This still makes the loggerhead the largest hard-shelled turtle, second among the sea turtles only to the massive leatherback. As with the other marine turtles, there are two subspecies composing the loggerhead species.

Although the carapace of the loggerhead is originally reddish-brown, it often becomes so worn, or so obscured by algae growths, that it is generally an undistinguished olive in maturity. The margins of the scutes may be, in their pristine state, a buttery yellow. Marginal yellow often occurs also in the limbs and tail and in the skin of the head. The main portion of the creature's skin, on both head and limbs, is usually dark, varying from red to chestnut brown.

The loggerhead is omnivorous, with a marked preference for meat. Their diet includes sponges, sea urchins, shrimp, jellyfish, oysters, mussels, conchs, barnacles, squid, crabs, and fish. Plants such as the ever popular, ever present turtle grass, as well as seaweed, are also consumed. Much of this food is collected from the bays, lagoons, and salt marshes of various shorelines. In addition, loggerheads frequent such spots as coral reefs and, according to Ernst and Barbour, shipwrecks, in search of sustenance. This makes good sense, for many of the creatures it prefers for food are also attracted to such underwater spots as wrecks or reefs.

The loggerheads are a particularly alert species. Although they are thought to spend a good deal of time just floating on the ocean's surface, any sort of disturbance will quickly spin them to action. They are also generally reported to have an aggressive, touchy character, and captives have reportedly gone after hands resting within their reach. Captives are also known for their territorial aggressiveness, selecting a spot in a pen or tank and defending it with powerful lunges at the intruding heads of other curious loggerheads. The idea that one of the world's greatest travelers is so addicted to territory seems very odd; I cannot help but wonder if their territorial behavior occurs only when the animal is placed in jarringly close confinement. Irritability under such conditions is understandable.

Although the loggerhead is both feisty and dangerous, it is hunted throughout its range for its meat and its prized eggs. In addition, many of its nesting sites in North America are being flattened and transformed into housing developments, hotels, and marinas. The raccoon shares man's liking for turtle eggs; and since the raccoon has been moving back into the coastlands it was once driven from, it is also contributing to the decline of the loggerhead. This wandering sea turtle once nested along many beaches in North America. Now, few undisturbed spots are left for it, and the likelihood of its continuing to nest on the continent is not good.

The ridley is the most modest of all sea turtles in appearance. *Lepidochelys kempii*, the Atlantic ridley, and *Lepidochelys olivacea*, the Pacific ridley, differ primarily in their muted coloration: the Atlantic ridley has a gray carapace, while the Pacific species has a distinctly olive one. Both have a heart-shaped carapace serrated along the posterior margin. The skin of the two ridleys follows the color of the shell, being either olive or gray. In both the head is wide, and the snout both wide and short. Males have long, stout tails. Females have much more abbreviated tails.

The Atlantic ridley occurs in North America from Newfoundland as far south as Bermuda. It is more closely associated with shallow coastal waters than the Pacific ridley, which is known to voyage far out into the Indian and Pacific Oceans. The Pacific ridley evidently often feeds in large bays and in the protected water found between coral reefs and shoreline. Both ridleys are generally carnivorous, feeding largely upon mollusks, crustaceans, jellyfish, and sea urchins; both also accept fish in captivity. There is some indication that the ridleys are predominantly bottom-feeders, preferring the oozy surface of the bottom for foraging (and concealment?).

The most nervous of the sea turtles, the ridley is capable of almost manic violence when captured. Although not large, it can devote remarkable strength to attacking those who attempt to lay hold of it. In captivity, ridleys may become calmer; but, reportedly, they never to lose their wariness and always sleep with their eyes open.

Dermochelys coriacea, the leatherback turtle, is the largest living reptile, as well as the largest extant species of turtle. The heftiest leatherback on record measured in at eight feet in length and an estimated weight of 1200 pounds. Certainly many other creatures, both on land and in the seas, are larger than the leatherback—but there is something terrificially distant about the leatherback, a sort of primal impressiveness. Viewed out of the water, as when the females come ashore to nest, the largest of the leatherbacks seem like the risen tenants of one's ancestral dreams, powerful, strange creatures having an incomprehensible, alien presence. The striking, unique design of *Dermochelys coriacea* adds much to this image.

The leatherback is alone among the marine turtles in lacking a shell. Instead, it has a smooth sheet of skin stretched across its back. This skin ranges from brown to black but may be flecked with a small number of white or yellow spots. The carapace is scaleless, triangular in shape, and distinguished by seven ridges that run its length from neck to tail. Great beefy shoulders and a large smooth head add to the visual impact of the turtle. The leatherback has a thick carpet of small bones beneath its smooth back, and in the taut skin of its back yet more small bones are wrapped. The limbs are dark, as is the head, aside from the gray upper jaw.

There is some debate whether the leatherback is properly divided into Atlantic and Pacific subspecies. It is argued that the two are so closely alike as to be virtually the same. That this point should still be unsettled is not surprising: very little is known of the leatherback, of its habits, its travels, its behavior. It is the most accomplished swimmer of all the sea turtles, and is thought to travel great distances through the oceans, far out of sight of any land.

Although it is known to eat jellyfish, seaweed, and algae, the leatherback is probably omnivorous, taking a variety of things whenever it can. Its omnivorous habits are well suited to its travels, for it occurs "throughout the tropical waters of the Atlantic, Pacific, and Indian oceans, from Newfoundland, the British Isles, British Columbia, and Japan south to Argentina, Chile, Australia, and the Cape of Good Hope. It also enters the Mediterranean Sea" (Ernst and Barbour, p. 250). It most likely feeds in the oceans, although it has been known to enter bays and other formations along the coastlines.

As befits this most mysterious of marine turtles, it does badly in captivity. Adults will batter themselves senseless attempting to escape from confinement, and will languish and die deprived of their freedom. Surprised in the oceans, leatherbacks have been known to put up vigorous, day-long battles in an attempt to escape, thrashing, avoiding ropes thrown over it to bind it, snapping off oars thrust at it, and emitting a loud, hoarse, angry roar.

Why would anyone *want* to capture a leatherback? For its oils, mostly. Although its flesh is occasionally sampled, it has the reputation of being unappetizing and sometimes poisonous. Even though it lacks a shell and yields no fat, the leatherback is valuable. The oils extracted from its skin—used for cosmetics and for varnish—have provided sufficient reason for hunting the massive turtle; unless this interest is curtailed, the animal will become extinct. Synthetic substitutes are readily available for the manufacture of the products for which the leatherback is killed.

The leatherback is already rare, occurring throughout its wide range in small numbers. There may be as few as 1000 mature females, perhaps even fewer, and it will not take much to push the species beyond the point of effective reproduction. That this most unusual, most wild of all sea turtles should perish for such trifling purposes is a bizarre comment on man's use of the natural world.

The Marshlands

The search for food must occasionally lead sea turtles from their usual feeding grounds offshore into the marshy fringes of the coastline. One wonders whether this search for sustenance might, on occasion, bring the sea turtles and the diamondback terrapin, *Malaclemys terrapin*, face to face. For the marshes, coves, estuaries, and tidal flats of the Atlantic coastline are the home range of the diamondback. It is an unusual and demanding environment, though a rich one, and the diamondback is the only species of turtle to successfully settle there.

Sea turtles and diamondbacks have something more in common than a shared ancestor. Both have suffered from the depredations of men. The records of the colonists who settled on the Atlantic coast in the sixteenth and seventeenth centuries indicate that diamondbacks must once have been very common. But, aside from its tasty flesh, the diamondback is of little interest to man. Most of its life is carried on out of human sight, as the salt marshes grant the diamondback a great degree of protection from all but the most determined of predators. The marsh is a curious habitat, for it is composed both of land and of fresh and salt water.

There are seven subspecies of diamondback. The variations that distinguish them are largely the result of their inhabiting different parts of the coastline. As the marshes are often broken up—and many long stretches of coastline no longer have marshes—the various populations of diamondbacks have been prevented from intermingling. *Malaclemys terrapin terrapin* ranges from Cape Cod to Cape Hatteras. *M.t. centrata* has a range that begins at Cape Hatteras and stretches south to the northern tip of Florida. *M. t. tequesta* Schwartz is found along Florida's Atlantic coastline. *M. t. rhizophorarum* Fowler is found only in the Florida Keys. *M. t. macrospilota* Hay is found along the Gulf coast of both Alabama and Florida. *M. t. pileata* occurs from Florida to Louisiana on the Gulf coast. *M. t. littoralis* Hay begins where *pileata* leaves off, in western Louisiana, and holds a range from there to western Texas. Imagine a line drawn along the North American coast from Cape Cod all the way down to the tip of Florida, then up Florida's other coast, along Louisiana, all the way to the western portion of the Texas coastline, almost to the tip of the Texas border's farthest point: such, once, was the range of the diamondback. While holding to a narrow strip, the terrapin was obviously a successful species. Judging by the records of the settlers along this area, it appears that all the subspecies were prolific, occurring in such great numbers because their habitat was rich enough to furnish food for all.

The diamondback's range thus includes all those parts of the coastline having brackish water—marshes, coves, tidal flats, estuaries, and those sheltered bodies of water behind barrier beaches. In such environments, the water is an admixture of salt and fresh. Diamondbacks have grown used to this combination. Whereas they do make journeys out to sea and up various streams and rivers that flow into the marshes, they usually sicken if kept for more than a few days in either purely salt or purely fresh water.

The markings on the carapace of the diamondback do not much remind me of diamond shapes, but they are quite handsome. Each scute on the carapace has a series of concentric ridges having a raised surface, set one within the other, all very clearly defined. The pattern may vary slightly among the subspecies. *M. t. macrospilota* has a bright yellow or orange wedge in the middle of each scute, giving the entire design of the carapace an even more pleasing aspect. *M. t. tequesta,* by contrast, lacks the series of ridges that the six other subspecies have. The carapace may be gray, brown, or black. The skin runs from a rather dark gray to black, and is usually marked throughout by a pattern of small light spots, giving it a very mottled effect. The head is short, narrow, and rather pointed. The skin above *M. t. terrapin's* upper lip is very dark, giving the distinct impression of a mustache, often lending the subspecies (in my opinion) a rather debonair and rakish look.

Diamondbacks are largely diurnal, often spending much of the morning basking on mud flats, or lying in muddy spots, perhaps half submerged under water, mud, and plants. Many hours are alternatively spent actively searching the marshes for food. Diamondbacks are omnivorous, taking snails, crabs, clams, marine worms, and marsh plants. They will also take insects when the opportunity arises. If carrion is available, they will take it.

During the winter they seek out the muddy bottoms of ponds and streams, or of tidal flats, and busy themselves in the mud. During warm spells they may emerge, rather groggily move about or feed, and seek out a muddy refuge when the weather turns chilly again.

Soon after the turtles emerge from their winter retreats, they actively search out members of the opposite sex for courtship and mating. Only when the females emerge from their usual habitat, to seek out nesting sites above the high tide mark, do diamondbacks become visible to the observer. At this point they become very vulnerable, both to accidents and to collection. Females have been known to lay eggs as often as five times a year, up to an average of 35 eggs for the year. These eggs, more delicate than those of some other turtle species, are easily destroyed by handling.

The diamondback is a small, attractive, and now elusive species, unfortunately depleted because of its good taste and by the destruction of its nesting sites and native habitats. Local populations may occasionally still be large; but much of its former range shows little or no sign of the diamondback. It may once have had some positive effect in controlling marshland populations of mosquitoes. It is hardly capable of having much effect now.

Fresh-Water Habitats

The fresh-water rivers, streams, lakes, and ponds of North America provide both the home and primary food source for most of the native species of turtles. The remarkable concentration of turtles in bodies of fresh water must have come about for a number of reasons. Chief among them is the abundance of plants and small edible creatures found in and around fresh water. Such life forms are present in great numbers and often easy to gather. In addition, water confers a special kind of mobility, making travel for turtles adapted to water both fast and relatively effortless. Water is also an excellent refuge, disguising turtles from those predators large enough to be interested in them, and also discouraging the curious. It is not surprising, then, that the majority of chelonian species in North America have settled in watery environments; only a few have remained primarily terrestrial.

Most people with whom I have spoken about the life in fresh waters assume that the ecosystems of rivers or lakes are relatively simple. But they are not. Each type—river, stream, pond, or lake—differs from the next in its composition and in the interaction of its parts. Some turtles fit into most of these habitats. Others prefer, and have specifically adapted to, life in one particular kind of fresh-water habitat.

Algae and other green plants are the commonest and the most important life forms in the continent's water. They compose the broad base of the aquatic pyramid of life. All other larger life forms depend, in some direct or indirect way, on the presence of the algae: a pond, a stream, or a river unable to support algae will be largely devoid of life. For many tiny creatures depend on the algae for food, and many bulkier creatures depend in turn on the algae-feeders. Lacking algae, the whole fragile web of aquatic

45

life is greatly weakened and may even collapse.

As plants, algae efficiently transform the energy of sunlight, carbon dioxide, and water into nutrients and oxygen. Both the end products are essential to the continuation and support of all life in an ecosystem. Only plants are capable of manufacturing their own nutrients; all other life forms must consume to get their food.

There are thousands of kinds of algae, almost all of them too tiny (individually) to be seen without the aid of a microscope. You cannot see *an* alga, but you can frequently *see* algae. In many watery habitats algae occur in such masses as to noticeably affect the color—turning the water a brilliant green, or coating every object (fallen trees, rocks, plants) along a stretch of water with a slippery brown or otherwise dark film. It is not unusual for aquatic turtles to sport a coat of algae on their shells. This is not, as is sometimes assumed, a sign of great age, for even a thick growth can spring up on the space of a few weeks. It does, however, give even a juvenile turtle the look of mossy old age.

Algae generally occur in colonies, either anchored to some current or drifting along in the current. Great amounts of other material are carried along on a current, just below or on the surface of the water. Much of this material is plankton—forms of algae and tiny creatures associated with it that normally float along, not anchored to a surface. Plankton is an important food source for aquatic creatures.

The plants and trees occurring along the banks of any body of fresh water play an important role in increasing the supply of nutrients to the water. Plant parts, including dead leaves that fall into the water, are sources of food for some insects, or are quickly dissolved by bacteria that release the nutrients of the debris for use by other creatures. In addition, masses of collected debris in water serve as a refuge for small creatures, encourage their proliferation, and thus indirectly serve to increase the supply of food for larger creatures.

The amount of plankton and other algae varies greatly from spot to spot, depending on the time of year, supplies of nutrients from the land, and the force of the current in a given location. At different times of the year the force may greatly increase or decrease, either carrying plankton along or allowing it to remain for some time in one area. The abundance or scarcity of the basic food supply largely determines the number of other creatures present. Aquatic turtles follow the food supply, browsing in an area until the supply becomes discouragingly skimpy, and then move on.

Because the majority of North American turtles share fresh-water environments, I have chosen to describe several species in some detail rather than cover lightly each of the many aquatic species. My intention is to indicate the kinds of adaptations that fresh-water habitats require; many of the essential facts would be needlessly repeated in a discussion of all the species.

Much of the life and behavior of *Clemmys muhlenbergii*, the bog turtle, is a mystery to us, and there is the possibility that it will remain so. The bog turtle inhabits marshy meadows and swamps and bogs generally associated with slow-moving streams that have soft bottoms but little sediment suspended in the water. This chelonian is in bad shape: its habitat has been everywhere claimed by men, in many places altered, in other places badly exploited; swamps and bogs have been stripped of saleable items, drained, and filled in. Perhaps never a very common turtle, *Clemmys muhlenbergii* is now positively rare. Muhlenberg's turtle, as it is also sometimes called, is so closely adapted to its environment that it cannot adjust to the changes now forced upon it. The U.S. Department of the Interior has placed the bog turtle on its list of rare and endangered species, and its name is likely to remain there until the species finally disappears. Only by strictly preserving those few untouched bogs and swamps where it has managed to hang on may it have a chance to survive.

For such a rare creature, the bog turtle is deceptively modest in appearance. It is small, shy, and has a rough brown or black carapace. Each scute has an indistinct smattering of a color, usually orange, towards its center. The skin is brown with a distinct admixture of orange or red. The most striking parts of its appearance are the bright patches of color (either red, yellow, or orange) located on either side of the head. The average length of a bog turtle is three-and-a-half inches. Some may reach four inches. A specimen measuring four-and-a-half inches established a record. Their diminutive size makes them one of the smallest of all North American turtle species. It also makes them terrifically inconspicuous.

Bog turtles have sharp claws, especially on their forelimbs. Powerful burrowers, they use their claws to quickly work down into the soft, thick mud found on the bottom of a bog. The claws may also come into play during the bog turtle's search for food. Bog turtles are basically omnivorous, taking both live prey and plants. Yet Robert Zappalorti, the Associate Curator of Herpetology at the Staten Island (N.Y.) zoo, has noted during his field studies a definite preference for live prey, including crayfish, crickets, bullfrogs, tadpoles, slugs, snails, and wood frogs. Zappalorti further notes that captive bog turtles, who disdain to eat prepared food, can always be tempted to feed by starting them off with live prey. They are bold aggressors, willing to tackle rather large creatures; and they are quite opportunistic, taking whatever comes their way in an indiscriminate fashion. Unlike fully aquatic turtles, bog turtles often prowl about on the land and eat their food either in or out of water (aquatic species can swallow food only when in water). They probably scavenge carrion, and also eat berries, seeds, and some plant material. For such small and wary chelonians, they are remarkably robust in their feeding habits.

The young are very secretive, taking shelter as soon as they have emerged from their eggs and remaining very wary until maturity. They have good reason for such caution, such practised elusive behavior: they are taken by raccoons, dogs, skunks, and some birds. Without great caution they could not survive. Generally more aquatic in their habits than adults, and more sensitive to hot weather, they remain under shelter when the days are especially warm.

Most of the time bog turtles are either basking or seeking food. They maintain burrows within a home range, but can quickly excavate a new one if they are startled away from shelter. During the sunniest days, bog turtles may bask and then begin searching out food quite early. On days less warm or less sunny, they may not cease basking until morning. At the hottest point of the day, they become less determined in their movements, perhaps even withdrawing until the worst is past. During the cold months they hibernate. Even during those months when it is active, the bog turtle is thought to spend the nights in a burrow, emerging only with the sunlight. Their burrows for hibernation may be located in relatively deep water. After emerging from their winter-long drowse, bog turtles evidently seek out upstream areas of less depth for feeding, mating, and nesting.

The map turtle, *Graptemys geographica*, presents an excellent example of species well adapted to life in the fresh waters of the continent. As with all truly aquatic species, it has very specific preferences within aquatic habitats. The map turtle does not frequent quiet ponds, gently flowing streams, or mid-current areas. It generally prefers large bodies of fresh water (lakes or rivers) and sites having abundant aquatic plants, soft thick muddy bottoms, and fallen logs or other debris that are useful as basking areas. Such locations are most often found close to the shore, perhaps in parts of a river somewhat protected from the full force of the current. The map turtle *likes* spacious bodies of water, so long as it can seek out the less powerful backwaters of a river or the quiet borders of a lake.

The common name of *Graptemys* was given for the thin, map-like yellow lines and circular markings of its brown carapace. Juveniles are more brilliantly marked than adults, a common occurrence among other species. Adult males retain the markings, though in a more subdued manner. Adult females generally lose the markings, passing through life with a simple brown or olive-colored carapace. There is a distinct, but low, ridge running from neck to tail along the middle of the carapace. The skin is the same olive or brown shade as the carapace, although it is considerably brightened by yellow stripes.

Map turtles spend most of the daylight hours basking on debris above the water or, occasionally, on land. While most other activities in a turtle's life call for individual action, basking is often communal, a chance for a comfortable gathering of otherwise standoffish individuals. Map turtles are especially noted for such behavior, crowding together onto every inch of surface of a spot. They are, for some reason, terrifically wary, and never more so than when basking. The smallest unknown noise, the slightest unusual disturbance, will cause them to plunge as one into the water and to seek out shelter below the surface.

With the onset of twilight, or at night, map turtles begin foraging for food. Fresh-water clams, crayfish, insects, and snails are taken. They may also scavenge from the carcasses of dead fish. Acquatic plants are also occasionally eaten. Feeding always takes place under water. Map turtles flush out their food by walking along the bottom and searching out the inhabitants of the clumps of plants.

The close identification with a particular habitat has had an adverse effect on many creatures. Map turtles are a case in point: the disruption and pollution of life in lakes and rivers has had a devastating effect on their populations. Poisons in the water destroy them directly. The fragility and susceptibility of their food sources to industrial effluents (or pesticides) pose an indirect threat to the map turtle's survival. Because of the remarkable wariness of this species (what is it they flee so precipitously from?), it is difficult to get an accurate account of their numbers or to collect them for study. Yet because of their habit of submerging at the slightest suspicious sound, map turtles have rarely been hunted for food. Nonetheless, they may be disappearing, forever, another victim of the casual, careless, continuing destruction of our rivers.

Three species of soft-shelled turtles occur in the fresh waters of the continent: the smooth softshell (*Trionyx muticus*), the spiny softshell (*Trionyx spiniferus*), and the Florida softshell (*Trionyx ferox*). A fourth, the Chinese softshell (*Trionyx sinensis*), has been introduced into the Hawaiian Islands as a source of food. Its natural range is exclusively Asian, including China, Formosa, and Vietnam.

I have heard the softshells referred to as "pancake" turtles, though I do not think this term is commonly used. Both it and the term softshell refer to the unique appearance of these chelonians, an appearance that is evidently the result of a number of specialized adaptations to life in the water. Softshells have low, round, rather flattened bodies. Instead of having distinct scutes, the carapace is covered by a seamless, tough layer of skin. This leathery coat would be enough to distinguish the softshells. However, their appearance is made considerably more startling because of a long neck and an elongated snout—a nose shaped into a long tubular extension at the end of which are the nostrils. No other kinds of turtles look so odd. Yet the softshells are not a line of bizarre failures, some evolutionary fumble. If anything, they are among the most closely adapted of all chelonians to their environment. The low, featureless shell allows them to settle into, and be disguised by, the soft muddy bottom of a stream or lake. The long neck allows a softshell to extend itself without moving, to take food at some remove from itself. The extended snout allows the turtle to remain motionless in the bottom of a shallow stream, to breathe without having to stir or surface. Frequently, softshells will lie motionless, settled into the mud, with just the top of the snout breaking the surface. Thus disguised, they have success in taking even some wary prey. Moreover, the streamlined form and powerful limbs of the softshell give it swiftness and agility.

T. muticus, the smooth softshell, is the most thoroughly aquatic of the American soft-shelled turtles. It will leave the water only when there is no alternative, or when necessity forces it—during, for instance, the season of nest-digging and egg-laying. The two subspecies of *T. muticus* occur over a remarkably wide range, from Pennsylvania west to Oklahoma, as far north as Wisconsin, as far south as Texas and Louisiana. Its range includes all or part of twenty states. While it prefers rivers and streams having a sustained current, it can also be found in lakes and other more shallow bodies of water. Whenever it occcurs, it prefers a location with a sandy bottom and few obstructions, such as rocks or thick clumps of underwater plants. Finding itself in a pool that is evaporating, the softshell will often burrow into the mud rather than go overland in search of other bodies of water. However, while a softshell dislikes land, it is a fast traveler, and is said to be able to outdistance a man.

You may find it a hard task to locate a softshell to race. They are shy and alert creatures, and they are carefully camouflaged. Both carapace and skin are a rather dull olive or orange. A white stripe, its margins outlined in black, extends from the skin around the eye to the neck. The feet are webbed and have claws, which facilitate the animal's distinct preference for meat. They take a variety of fish, frogs, crayfish, snails, aquatic insects, and tadpoles. There is one report of a softshell overtaking a brook trout, one of the fastest of all North American fresh-water fish. When not lying concealed, and waiting for its prey to approach it, the smooth softshell will seek out food by prowling along the bottom of a waterway, either swimming or walking. The temper of the softshell is a matter still unresolved; there are differing opinions on the subject. A softshell may respond with timidity to human inspection; but it may also snap. In its attempt to escape, its sharp claws could inadvertently leave one's flesh severely scored. Picking up a softshell can panic the turtle and easily cause the handler further damage. Nonetheless, softshells are everywhere taken for food. If properly prepared, their flesh is said to be quite savory.

All of the softshells bask for up to several hours a day. The smooth softshell will stretch itself out when basking, extending its limbs and stretching its neck to its full length. If no projection in the water is available, softshells will come ashore to bask. But they will stay in a spot close to the water, facing it, with no obstructions to sight or escape. They remain alert throughout this necessary exercise; if their suspicion is in any way aroused, they will streak back to the water, entering and disappearing in one motion.

The spiny softshell, *T. spiniferus,* is more distinctly marked than the smooth softshell. A think black line appears along the margins of the carapace. The surface of the olive or tan carapace is distinguished by a random pattern of dark blotches. The blotches may be dark throughout or dark on the margins and lighter toward the center of the spot (rather like gobs of ink spattered onto water). The olive-colored head and limbs continue this pattern of spots. As with the smooth softshell, the nose is snout-like, the feet webbed and clawed. The spiny softshell is a highly aquatic species. Most of its time is spent prowling the bottom, floating about the surface of the water, or buried in the muddy bottom of some shallow point waiting for prey to pass by. It is decidedly carnivorous, taking crayfish, fish, frogs, insects, mollusks, and tadpoles. Food may be swallowed whole or torn into pieces by its sharp jaws while clasped by the even sharper claws of the forelimbs. Spiny softshells sometimes nose out food beneath rocks or in clumps of plants, using their snouts to overturn rocks and part strands of plants in the manner of a dog investigating interesting scents.

There are six subspecies of the spiny softshell covering a range that includes some thirty-six states and several Canadian provinces, reaching as far north as Quebec and Ontario, as far south as the entire Gulf Coast, as far west as Arizona. As its range indicates, this is a very successful turtle. Part of the reason for this is its adaptability to various habitats. It can be found in "marshy creeks, large swift-flowing rivers, bayous, oxbows, lakes and impoundments" (Ernst and Barbour, p. 262). The spiny softshells like a rather tangled underwater scene, where aquatic plants, limbs of fallen trees, and other debris combine to produce a diverse environment. A soft bottom, for purposes of disguise, is essential; and if a sandbar is nearby, for safe basking, so much the better.

Trionyx ferox, the Florida softshell, has a more leathery carapace than the other soft-shells. Along the edges of the carapace, and occasionally elsewhere on it, are large knobby bumps. The coloration of the carapace is rather indistinct, being generally brown or gray-brown, with a vague suggestion of a lighter brown intermixed: the whole effect reminds me of something seen out of focus, as if one were staring at an object obscured by the ripples of disturbed water. This effect must make very good camouflage in the Florida softshell's murky environment, which includes habitats having "deep water with sand or mud bottoms, or bubbling mud-sand springs where there is foliage overhead" (Ernst and Barbour, p. 267). It is found from the southern tip of South Carolina throughout the southeastern portion of Georgia and all the way through Florida.

Like the other soft-shells, *T. ferox* spends its days alternately looking for food, floating on the surface, or basking. It may be slightly less carnivorous than the other softshells, eating some plants when other food is unavailable. However, the bulk of its diet is evidently composed of crayfish, fish, frogs, mussels, and snails. The Florida softshell is a burrower, a frequent denizen of the mud. It seeks out the muddy bottoms and roots down into the stuff until only its neck and head are visible. Curiously, *T. ferox* is apparently so convinced of its invisibility in such situations that it can be handled with impunity: it must dismiss the intrusion as being unrelated to itself. It is also able to excavate mud and tunnel through it with astonishing speed.

The Woodlands

A life lived almost entirely on land has its own particular pressures and demands. The box turtle, *Terrapene carolina,* and the wood turtle, *Clemmys insculpta,* are the two kinds of turtles associated primarily with terrestrial habitats, although both will also enter the water.

The markings on the shells of several subspecies of box turtle are quite handsome, being either very subtle but distinct, or quite bold and bright. Wood turtles have a more unusual shell. It is broad, rather low overall, and reminds me of nothing so much as a series of large sea shells laid across the back to form a rough mosaic. In fact, each scute is raised into an "irregular pyramid," as Ernst and Barbour describe it, forming "a series of concentric growth-ridges and grooves" (p. 80). The ridges are noticeably raised, giving the shell a striking roughness and the impression of a fluid, balanced design.

Of the two kinds of turtles, the wood turtle is probably more given to rambling than the box turtle. *Clemmys insculpta* has been observed in open woodland, around marshes and bogs, and in pastureland. It has a greater preference for water than the box turtle, often visiting bodies of fresh water such as streams and pools. The wood turtle seems to prefer copulating in the water, and frequently swims out to logs or rocks in midstream for morning basking.

It is active throughout the day from the end of March to the middle of October. When the weather turns colder in the fall, it seeks out a hibernation site in some muddy pond bottom or vacant burrow excavated by another creature in the lower bank of a stream. The wood turtle is not gregarious, and aside from the mating period prefers to go its solitary way. It is not, however, pugnacious; contacts with its own kind do not result in violence.

Wood turtles are omnivorous. In this there is little choice: because of the fluctuation in the supply of various food items, some being plentiful as others become exhausted, wood turtles cannot afford to depend on just one or two food sources. They are known to eat grasses, algae from ponds or streams, leaves, sorrel, and berries. Earthworms, insects, mollusks, and tadpoles are also consumed; and the wood turtle may sometimes act as a scavenger of small dead mammals and birds. Ernst and Barbour report that "captives readily eat apples and canned dog food," and that they "relish hard-boiled eggs" (p. 83). During times of scarcity on land, wood turtles will turn back to the water and spend most of their time there searching for food.

The wood turtle would be sufficiently distinguished just by its success in a difficult environment. However, it has been claimed on the wood turtle's behalf that it is the most intelligent of all turtles. It is certainly among the most repsonsive to humans. Its ability to learn has been established as "about equal" with a rat's. This distinction, Archie Carr notes "has a rather uncomplimentary ring," but "is really pretty good for a turtle; and anyway, in a personality contest a wood turtle would win from a rat in a walk" (p. 121). Josephine Knowlton, author of the delightful book *My Turtles,* and, according to Carr, a woman who "probably knows more about the subjective attributes of a number of species of turtles than does anyone alive," stated that the wood turtle was the most intelligent species of turtle she had ever encountered. Wood turtles are long-lived and have a remarkably extroverted character. They seem to be aware of the actions of humans, capable of adapting to them, to the extent which they find necessary. Carr describes a "sprightly female that we kept in the house for eighteen months [who] soon learned as much as interested her of our daily routine. She slept in a closet and showed up at the breakfast table every morning where she made for my wife's chair, craned her neck expectantly, and often stood on three legs with one front foot lifted and poised like a pointer dog that smells birds." (Pp. 121-122.)

Josephine Knowlton had a wood turtle (again a female) that would frequently stand upon its hind legs to beg for food. Ernst and Barbour note that the wood turtle has real ability as a climber, and that they once observed a wood turtle climbing a chain link fence—no mean feat. This is rather a mixed bag of incidents, but they do all seem to indicate a shrewd and adaptable nature, combined with some power of observation.

All of this would seem to make the wood turtle the most desirable sort of chelonian for a pet. Unfortunately, the wood turtle is in trouble in much of its range owing to the destruction of both land and water habitats and to their propensity for trying to cross roads, oblivious to the traffic bearing down upon them. In parts of its range the wood turtle has been declared an endangered species, making it illegal to collect and keep them in captivity. A further problem may be the ingestion of pesticides which have drained into water systems from fields have or been absorbed by insects that the wood turtle eats. The range of effects pesticides have on turtles has not yet been thoroughly investigated, but one can assume that a buildup of pesticides in a turtle's fat is not beneficial.

Box turtles are more restricted in their range than wood turtles. They travel less frequently and for shorter distances. Indeed, they are far more abundant than wood turtles, and they occur through a much larger portion of the continent. The common names of the subspecies—the eastern box turtle, the Gulf Coast box turtle, and the Florida box turtle—indicate a good deal about their range. The fourth subspecies, usually referred to as the three-toed box turtle, also occurs throughout the south, from Missouri to Alabama, and west to Texas. While it can be found in pastures and in meadows, the box turtle clearly prefers open woodlands.

During the warmest months of the year, box turtles are active only in the morning or after a rain shower. During the warmest hours of the day, they take refuge in abandoned burrows, in mud, under rotten logs, or in masses of decaying organic matter. They may also find puddles or small pools and remain motionless in them throughout the afternoon.

In belief, if not in fact, this is our most common turtle. When you mention turtles to people, the first species many are likely to think of will be box turtles. And when you question people about the pets they kept as children, many are again likely to mention a favorite box turtle. The box turtle may have attained this status because, being terrestrial, it is highly visible; or, because it does not have a particularly wary nature and will not hide from man, as some of the fresh-water species do.

Deserts: The Desert Tortoise

The intense heat and lack of accessible water make deserts hard environments. Yet they are far from lifeless. All but the grimmest of deserts (such as Death Valley or, in Asia, the Gobi Desert) are home for a wide variety of plants and small animals. To survive the intense heat, animals have had to regulate their periods of greatest activity to coincide with the period when the heat is least intense: the night. Most desert creatures are nocturnal. They are also, usually, quite small. A smaller body requires less water. And it can also more easily find shelter.

For during the hours when the sunlight is most intense, the heat most appalling, shelter must be taken. It could be said that the adaptation of animals to the heat is to hide from it. The other great challenge confronting desert animals is the need for water. Most species have met this difficulty by adjusting their physiology both to conserve water and to make do with less.

The desert tortoise, *Gopherus agassizii*, provides an excellent example of the wide-range of adjustments that chelonians necessarily have had to make in order to survive in such an environment.

Gopherus agassizii is a large tortoise, characterized by extraordinarily large hind feet and a rough carapace with a serrated edge along the rear. A ridge of shell projects forward from the plastron, forming a shield for the underside of the neck. The shell ranges from dark tan to black, with light but noticeable patches of yellow or orange in the center of the scutes of the carapace. The color of the skin on the head varies from tan to powdery red. The neck is often rather yellow, and the skin on the limbs is brown. The texture of the skin is rough; the skin consists of a pattern of thick, overlapping scales.

Those parts of a desert having both sandy soil and scrub creosote bushes or cacti are its habitat. Unlike most other North American chelonians, the desert tortoise exacvates a burrow and settles into a life centered around this refuge. The burrows are always dug in a dry soil that is either sandy or very gravelly. The tortoise chooses a spot beneath a bush, in a bank, or at the base of a cliff. It uses the thick claws on its forelegs to scrape out the soil. There is remarkable variation in the design of the burrow. Some desert tortoises dig burrows just big enough to wedge themselves in. Others excavate chambers up to 30 feet in length. Burrows may be straight, leading downwards; or they may be curved; or forked. And they may feature enlarged chambers.

At least in some parts of its range (notably in Utah), desert tortoises dig two different kinds of burrows: shallow holes into which they retreat during the hottest days of the year, and deep dens of from 8 to 30 feet for hibernation. The burrows are not simply retreats to shield the tortoises from the Sun; they are a very efficient means of controlling the climate. Within a burrow there is more humidity and a much lower more constant temperature than on the surface. Only a few inches below the desert surface, the temperature on even the hottest of days may be no more than 90°F. (By contrast, the temperature on the surface may climb far above 100°F.) On the hottest days, the tortoise may remain in its burrow. In less devastating weather, the tortoise will forage for food for a brief period after sunrise and again in the late afternoon. Unlike many other desert creatures, it is not nocturnal. Throughout its range, the desert tortoise hibernates from October, or November, to March. Tortoises often congregate in large clans. Ernst and Barbour cite one report of a communal burrow containing 23 tortoises. These dens were frequently enlarged ground-squirrel burrows, although tortoises have been observed to cooperatively excavate a site.

The desert tortoise has adjusted to the intense heat of its environment by moving underground. It has developed a variety of responses to the chronic undersupply of water in a desert. In some parts of its range, rains may come as infrequently as every few years. When water is available, tortoises will accept it. But the primary source of moisture for tortoises is their food. Tortoises are largely herbivorous, consuming various desert plants and grasses. However, in captivity they do accept snails and insects as food. The plants they consume contain some moisture. From such a diet tortoises derive most of the minimal amount of moisture they need to survive. Another source is their own bodily oxidation, which produces water in the tissues from the breakdown of food. Moreover, the skin of desert tortoises allows less moisture to evaporate than the skin of turtles in climates having greater amounts of moisture.

While tortoises tend to inhabit small, fixed territories during their active months, migrations do occur when conditions in an area become unfavorable. The desert tortoise may never have been very common, for it takes upwards of 10 acres to supply sufficient food for one tortoise. However, given the harsh conditions of the environment its ancestors wandered into, the tortoise has adjusted very well. A large population is not always the sign of success. A stable population, matching the food supply of an area, is.

Desert tortoises are not sexually mature until they are from 15 to 20 years old. The males, usually placid creatures, become irritable and aggressive during the mating season. It is usual, when two tortoises meet, for them to nod their heads rapidly, and perhaps even touch noses, before they resume their respective journeys. However, when two males meet during the mating season, a fight usually ensues. They will first draw back, then rush towards one another, each using the ridge of shell projecting forward from the plastron to butt one another. The projection may also help to tip an antagonist over; it often takes some time for the loser to right himself.

Courtship is equally aggressive. During the spring males will seek out and approach females, nodding the head in a rapid up-and-down pattern. As he draws close, the male may nip at the female's shell, at her forelegs, or even at her nose. Such violence does not deter the female: in some cases females have been seen to initiate courtship. (But at least one captive female has been observed giving a captive male a thorough thumping and forcing the male to withdraw into its shell.) The male mounts the female from the rear, taking an almost erect stance, resting his forelimbs on her shell. His lovemaking is accompanied by very audible sighs and groans, lending the act an unsettling, very human quality.

Nests are excavated and eggs laid by the females during the latter half of May and into July. The female uses her hind limbs to excavate a nest in sandy soil. The nest is usually wide at the top, narrowing towards the bottom. She also employs her hind limbs to deftly arrange the eggs in the nest. An average of five eggs are laid per nest, and each female may lay up to three clutches in a season. It requires about 100 days for the hatchlings to develop and emerge. When they do, they come out fighting. Hatchlings carry a pose of aggressiveness with them—something their elders adopt only during the mating process. The young tortoises are almost as wide as they are long. Their low, flat profile, and the dull brown or yellow shade of the carapace, with darker brown markings on each scute, serve somewhat to camouflage them. But coyotes, ravens, and bobcats do often find and eat the hatchlings; and foxes, hawks, and skunks may be their predators too.

Gopherus berlandieri, the Texas tortoise, is found throughout southern Texas. Its range extends into several Mexican states. While it prefers scrub woods having sandy, well-drained soil, it also inhabits a variety of habitats occurring in southern Texas, from near-desert conditions to rather humid, even sub-tropical, areas. It is smaller than the desert tortoise; but its shell, with roughly-ridged scutes having bright yellow centers, greatly resembles the shell of its relative. The skin is yellowish and the face more pointed than that of the desert tortoise.

Unlike either the desert or gopher tortoise, the Texas tortoise does not dig burrows. Intead, it simply pushes away the surface soil of a spot, creating a slight depression into which it will settle to rest. Such depressions, referred to as pallets, are usually found at the edge of clumps of cactus, or under special kinds of bushes. As with desert tortoises, the Texas tortoise has adapted to habitats having little surface water by taking much of the moisture it needs from its food. All three species of North American tortoises also have the ability to reabsorb water from their bladder, and excrete their urine as a semisolid. (Herpetologists disagree just how important this adaptation is to a tortoise's survival.) The Texas tortoise is largely herbivorous, feeding on the flowers and fruit of cacti, various grasses, and some plants.

In a rare reversal of the usual rule, some human activities actually benefit the tortoise. Areas which have been cleared of brush and opened to grazing by cattle achieve a level and density of brush ideal for the tortoises. In addition, grazing encourages the growth of prickly pear, a favorite food of the tortoises. Once taken heavily for the pet trade, the Texas tortoise is now protected and may be able to maintain a stable population within its range. Yet the automobile continues to take its toll of tortoises attempting to cross roads.

Gopherus polyphemus, the gopher tortoise, looks much like the desert and Texas tortoises. Its shell is very similar. It differs in having skin of a grayish-black hue. Somewhat larger than the Texas tortoise, it is usually about the size of the desert tortoise. It is found along the southern coast from South Carolina to Florida, and west along the gulf coast to Louisiana. Its preference in habitats is unlike that of its relatives: it is most often found in the transitional zones between two ecosystems such as woodland and pasture. It is much more adapted to digging than the other tortoises, having immovable wrists that give its forelimbs a shovel-like movement and great power. It digs a long burrow, which it makes a permanent home and therefore takes some pains to keep free of debris. The very stable temperature and humidity within the burrow protect the tortoise from the alterations of climate occurring on the surface. Because the weather in their environment is cooler and more humid, gopher tortoises can remain active throughout the hottest hours of the day. And they remain active all year, going into a shortened hibernation only if the weather becomes momentarily severe.

Gopher tortoises are generally herbivorous; they eat grass, leaves, and wild fruit. However, they may also eat some insects, and in captivity they readily accept meat. A slow but steady swimmer, the gopher tortoise may sometimes search for food around bodies of water. Although the tortoise has occasionally been eaten, it is rarely taken for that purpose. According to Ernst and Barbour, it was once used by certain Indian tribes as a form of money, given and taken in trade. Its shell was used for both baskets and pots.

The Prairies

The prairies are characterized by long stretches of low hills, few trees or widely separated pieces of woodland, and seasons in which the temperatures can become quite harsh. What separates the prairie from all other habitats are the grasses: grass dominates the prairie. By supporting a great diversity of life, grass makes the prairie a complex, successful habitat. Before the advent of settlers, the prairie was the single largest ecosystem in North America, stretching from Canada down to Texas, and from the midwest far into the western regions. The only species of North American turtle to live predominantly in the prairie lands of the midwest and southwest is the ornate box turtle, *Terrapene ornata.*

The ornate box turtle is small but, because of the markings of its carapace, quite visible. The scutes are dark brown or tinged a red-brown; on each scute there are boldly drawn thick yellow streaks. Frequently, a broken yellow stripe will run the length of the center of the carapace. The dark brown skin is mottled with yellow spots, and the markings are repeated on the plastron—an unusual feature in turtles. Even the tail may have a series of small yellow stripes running along the center. It is as if the turtle were dazzled by the idea of such streaks being daubed on every possible surface.

While I have been unable to find any authoritative speculation on the origin of these markings, possibly they serve the purpose of camouflage. The patterns of blotches and stripes of color, found on turtles, mixed with the basic, predominantly dull colors of their skin or shells, is referred to as "disruptive." Such patterns, which seem so bold and even outlandishly colorful in captive animals, provide superb disguise in a turtle's natural setting. The habitats in which turtles move, either aquatic or terrestrial, are rarely brilliantly illuminated. Instead, the worlds of prairies, streams, and lakes are dappled with light in an uneven manner. Trees, grasses, the contours of the land, and water all interrupt the light, causing it to reach the ground or the areas beneath the water surface in a manner that is forever changing, illuminating some areas and leaving others in darkness. Under such conditions, the markings of a turtle are excellent camouflage, allowing a turtle lying motionless to appear simply as another inanimate object struck by random streaks of light.

Like many other small creatures of the prairies, the ornate box turtle has had to become a digger in the earth to survive the extreme temperatures characteristic of prairie land. They are most active in the cool mornings and during the late afternoons, sheltering in a burrow throughout the warmest hours of the day. This is not because the turtles dislike sunlight. During the morning hours, ornate box turtles do some basking. But exposure to the heat of the midday sun is quickly fatal: the turtles just cannot compensate for such a rapid rise in temperature. The burrow may be one they have excavated, or one they have discovered, a hole abandoned by some other tenant. Ornate turtles may also seek shelter under bushes, or, during the hottest summer days, in pools of water. In an area having winters that are often harsh, hibernation is essential. Ornate turtles begin searching out a refuge, or excavating their own, in October; and by November they will enter into a winter's sleep.

Soon after the emergence from hibernation, the ornate box turtle begins courtship procedures. It is evidently not uncommon for several males to pursue one female. The usual ritual seems to call for the male to nudge the rear margins of the female's shell. After a certain point, when the male evidently deems the female to be receptive (or perhaps when he becomes desperate?), he will gather speed and literally hurl himself onto the female's back. The act of generation may last for up to two hours.

Females seem very particular when selecting a nesting site. They have been known to wander for as much as a week, pawing away at various spots and then moving on. What they are looking for is a place that is open, has good drainage, and that has soft, loosely textured soil. The female usually does not begin the next until the evening, and does not finish it until after dark. She may empty her bladder to soften the soil on the surface and in the nest itself. A moist nest is essential: warmth without humidity will soon destroy a clutch, which normally numbers from two to eight eggs. The hatchlings are taken by such predators as hawks, coyotes, crows, skunks, and some snakes. The young are understandably elusive, and at least one investigator has suggested that they spend the early part of their lives in burrows, subsisting on the insects to be found in and around such spots.

An early dependence on insects may explain the preference most ornate box turtles seem to show for insects as a primary food source throughout their lives. Beetles, grasshoppers, and caterpillars seem to be the most favored kinds. Dung beetles may be the single most important item; the disturbance of balls of dung is a sure sign of an ornate box turtle's foraging for food. Plants and berries are also eaten, sometimes in quantity. Ornate box turtles have been observed in the wild scavaging carrion. Captive turtles have been observed to capture and eat tadpoles. Captives have also been seen to eat small pebbles. It is unclear why this is done, what purpose it could serve.

The continual transformation of prairie into farmland, and the numbers of turtles killed every year by automobiles, have affected the species. In addition, there is the problem posed by pesticides, which farmers use to control pest populations; some of these poisons make their way into the water sources in an area. Over a long period of time, such ingested poisons may accumulate until they reach a dangerous level in a turtle's layer of fat. This may prove fatal or may diminish the ability of the species to lay eggs having sufficiently hard shells.

Although the extent of their influence cannot be determined, ornate box turtles are important in eating harmful insects. Their burrows may provide shelter for a variety of other creatures, thus encouraging the proliferation and success of life in a complex, but fragile, ecosystem. Should they quietly dwindle, and finally disappear, their going will surely further unsettle an environment that has already become less balanced, less complex, less rich, than once it was.

It is impossible to restore an ecosystem once it has been disturbed: far too complex a thing is it for us to understand, let alone match. However, it is still possible for us to preserve what is left, to reduce the pressures we are placing upon it, to take steps to save the remaining wildlife. Preserving the prairie as a functioning ecosystem benefits both man and the turtle: the boldly designed ornate box turtle, so mild and retiring in disposition, certainly deserves the chance.

On Observing Turtles in Their Natural Habitats

Given the choice of going out to catch turtles, or to watch them, I'd much prefer just looking. When you're intent on snaring a turtle, when the focus of your efforts is making a catch, you miss a good deal of what's going on. But when you're out just to study the behavior of turtles, you're free to investigate many supplementary matters, to listen, look, touch, and smell anything of interest around you. When you're studying turtles, you're bound to learn a good deal about all the other components of the creature's habitat: the plants, the configuration of the land, the interaction of the other inhabitants.

The word "natural" is used advisedly in the title above, for you can find turtles in many decidedly tame places, in urban and suburban areas, in local parks, in recreational areas. You needn't trek into the wilderness to find turtles. However, to find a sufficiently large population of turtles to watch and compare, you probably will have to seek out a relatively undisturbed spot. State, natural, or provincial parks are the best place to begin. They generally include a variety of habitats and are the only sites in which the land and its creatures are protected from most kinds of exploitation and pollution. There you are most likely to find stable populations of turtles. And there, with fewer interruptions, the turtles are more likely to pursue the necessary business of the day, having little to force them to shelter or cause them to be unusually wary.

Before you go out, you should of course become conversant with the appearance of the species likely to occur in your chosen site. Knowing something of their behavior patterns and preferred foods will be invaluable in helping you locate a species. When you're out there, what you'll need most is alertness matched with patience. You may choose to prowl along a likely area, such as a meadow, the margins of a body of water, or a stretch of swampland. Or you may want just to select a likely spot and stay put. Either way, you'll have to spend some time at it before getting results. If one site doesn't workout, keep looking. And ask around. Local people are often a source of valuable information. Most importantly, enjoy yourself. I've seen amateur researchers in the field who appear driven by a fierce determination to *do* something, to gather proof, to make a point. Very commendable. But being so resolutely focused often causes you to miss much, to enjoy little.

You may go out with a definite research project in mind. Or you may just want to be there to look, to savor the variety of pleasures one finds in any natural setting. Why rush the matter? You'll learn most by establishing a slow, steady pace, and by sticking to it—by being turtle-like in your plans and turtle-like in your methods.

There are a few necessary tools and study-aids that you should take along when you set out. A notebook is essential for recording what you see. A map of the study is necessary unless the terrain is familiar. If the area is very wild, or far removed from homes or park offices, take along a compass and master its use; for, when used in connection with an accurate map, it can be most helpful in leading you through unfamiliar territory. A small first-aid kit is also worth the extra weight. A camera will of course enable you to keep an accurate record of what you've seen; if fitted with a telescopic lens, it can serve as a stand-in for a pair of binoculars. A hand lens (magnifying glass) will allow you to closely investigate the markings on a carapace or the texture of skin, to study plants and other foodstuffs, and to bring into focus all those small, fine structures that are beyond your powers of visual discrimination. If you intend to examine turtles found in the wild, and then release them, a measuring tape will be needed to record their size. And if you're interested in identifying the plants you've observed turtles feeding on, you'll need some small bags to carry specimens home.

All of this may seem obvious; but it bears mention. There are no arcane mysteries to studying wildlife. The more complex equipment and procedures of ecologists, zoologists, and experienced naturalists are used to develop very specific data. But the basic act remains non-action: sitting, looking, and listening until you feel as much a part of the scene as any of its other inhabitants. You cannot force a landscape or a creature to reveal itself to you, to reduce itself to a finite plan. But you can become conversant with it by relinquishing any intention of controlling it, by respecting its behavior, and by becoming, equally, a transient part of its habitat.

Species of North American Turtles

Following is a list of the common and scientific names of each of the species of North American turles, and an identification of the primary habitat of each. The list is alphabetical, according to the common names of the species. Many of the species have several subspecies, each differing from the next only slightly in matters of coloration. Every subspecies of a species has the same preference in habitat. A thorough description of each species and subspecies can be found in the books recommended in the Bibliography.

(A) AQUATIC (FRESH-WATER) SPECIES
(M) MARINE (SEA-GOING) SPECIES
(T) TERRESTRIAL SPECIES

Common Name	Scientific Name	Primary Habitat	
Alabama map turtle	*Graptemys pulchra*	(A)	deep water, rivers
Alabama red-bellied turtle	*Chrysemys alabamaensis*	(A)	salt marshes, coastal swamps
Alligator snapping turtle	*Macroclemys temminckii*	(A)	rivers, lakes
Atlantic ridley	*Lepidochelys kempii*	(M)	shallow waters near coast
Barbour's map turtle	*Graptemys barbouri*	(A)	clear streams
Black-knobbed sawback	*Graptemys nigrinoda*	(A)	streams having sand or clay bottoms
Blanding's turtle	*Emydoidea blandingii*	(A)	shallow waters of lakes, ponds, marshes, creeks
Bog turtle	*Clemmys muhlenbergii*	(A)	bogs, marshes, swamps
Box turtle	*Terrapene carolina*	(T)	pastures, meadows, green woodlands
Chicken turtle	*Deirochelys reticularia*	(A)	still water, ponds, cypress swamps
Chinese softshell	*Trionyx sinensis*	(A)	marshlands, small streams
Cooter	*Chrysemys floridana*	(A)	any fresh-water body with slow current
Desert tortoise	*Gopherus agassizii*	(T)	desert habitat
Diamondback terrapin	*Malaclemys terrapin*	(A)	coastal marches, tidal flats
False map turtle	*Graptemys pseudogeographica*	(A)	lakes, ponds, large rivers
Florida red-bellied turtle	*Chrysemys nelsoni*	(A)	lakes, marshes, ponds
Florida snapping turtle	*Chelydra osceola*	(A)	fresh-water bodies with soft bottoms and abundant vegetation
Florida softshell	*Trionyx ferox*	(A)	all fresh-water habitats
Gopher tortoise	*Gopherus polyphemus*	(T)	transitional terrestrial areas
Green turtle	*Chelonia mydas*	(M)	throughout open seas
Hawksbill	*Eretmochelys imbricata*	(M)	shallow rocky areas, coral reefs
Leatherback	*Dermochelys coriacea*	(M)	throughout ocean

Common Name	Scientific Name		Primary Habitat
Loggerhead	*Caretta caretta*	(M)	throughout ocean
Loggerhead musk turtle	*Sternotherus minor*	(A)	rivers, streams, creeks, swamps
Map turtle	*Graptemys geographica*	(A)	rivers, lakes, ponds
Mississippi map turtle	*Graptemys kohnii*	(A)	lakes, rivers, sloughs
Mud turtle	*Kinosternon subrubrum*	(A)	shallow waters
Ornate box turtle	*Terrapene ornata*	(T)	prairies
Pacific ridley	*Lepidochelys olivacea*	(M)	open ocean and shallow waters
Painted turtle	*Chrysemys picta*	(A)	slow-moving shallow waters
Pond slider	*Chrysemys scripta*	(A)	any quiet fresh-water body
Razor-backed musk turtle	*Sternotherus carinatus*	(A)	rivers, streams, swamps
Red-bellied turtle	*Chrysemys rubriventris*	(A)	large, deep fresh-water bodies
Ringed sawback	*Graptemys oculifera*	(A)	rivers
River cooter	*Chrysemys concinna*	(A)	rivers, lakes, ponds
Rough-footed mud turtle	*Kinosternon hirtipes*	(A)	lakes, ponds in mesquite grasslands
Smooth softshell	*Trionyx muticus*	(A)	rivers, lakes, streams
Snapping turtle	*Chelydra serpentina*	(A)	all fresh-water bodies
Sonora mud turtle	*Kinosternon sonoriense*	(A)	creeks, rivers, ponds, springs
Spiny softshell	*Trionyx spiniferus*	(A)	creeks, rivers, lakes
Spotted turtle	*Clemmys guttata*	(A)	primarily bogs, streams; also land
Stinkpot	*Sternotherus odoratus*	(A)	rivers, ponds, lakes, streams
Striped mud turtle	*Kinosternon baurii*	(A)	ponds, swamps, quiet waters
Texas map turtle	*Graptemys versa*	(A)	lakes, ponds
Texas tortoise	*Gopherus berlandieri*	(T)	various deserts, woods
Western pond turtle	*Clemmys marmorata*	(A)	ponds, streams
Wood turtle	*Clemmys insculpta*	(T)	woods, fields, bogs
Yellow-blotched sawback	*Graptemys flavimaculata*	(A)	streams with sand or clay bottoms
Yellow mud turtle	*Kinosternon flavescens*	(A)	any quiet fresh-water habitat

Portfolio

Turtles have always been considered fit subjects for illustration, even when they weren't regarded with much more than passing interest in any other way. John White, a late sixteenth-century artist from the land of Virginia, included among his renderings of North American wildlife several exquisite watercolors of turtles. Since those first modern works, turtles have frequently been rendered by various American illustrators. The reason for this, I suspect, is quite simple. Many species of North American turtles have carapaces distinguished by brightly-colored designs or distinct symmetrical patterns. Their striking shell designs, moreover, are complemented by streaks or blotches of color on the limbs, necks, or heads of many species.

We have kept this often-stunning pictorial effect in mind when selecting the species to be illustrated for this book. However, the primary factors in the selection of subjects were their frequency of occurrence and their visibility. Many of the turtles in this portfolio are among the commonest, and most often seen, of all the North American species. It was our intention to make their identification easier for you, and our hope that these paintings will stimulate your rediscovery of the unique appeal embodied in chelonian form.

List of Color Plates

Plate I	Eastern Painted Turtle	*Chrysemys picta picta*
Plate II	Red-Eared Turtle	*Chrysemys scripta elegans*
Plate III	Florida Box Turtle	*Terrapene carolina bauri*
Plate IV	Northern Diamondback Terrapin	*Malaclemys terrapin terrapin*
Plate V	Yellow-Bellied Turtle	*Chrysemys scripta scripta*
Plate VI	Yellow Mud Turtle	*Kinosternon flavescens flavescens*
Plate VII	Wood Turtle	*Clemmys insculpta*
Plate VIII	Eastern Mud Turtle	*Kinosternon subrubrum subrubrum*
Plate IX	Southern Painted Turtle	*Chrysemys picta dorsalis*
Plate X	Map Turtle	*Graptemys geographica*
Plate XI	Alabama Map Turtle	*Graptemys pulchra*
Plate XII	The Life Cycle of Turtles	
Plate XIII	Eastern Box Turtle	*Terrapene carolina carolina*

Eastern Painted Turtle

Chrysemys picta picta

Like the other subspecies of painted turtles, the eastern painted turtle is diurnal, dividing the day into periods of foraging and basking. Basking is often carried on in large groups. Courtship behavior is particularly gentle; the male uses his foreclaws to stroke or caress the neck and head of the female. It is believed that painted turtles travel regularly between a series of bodies of water to facilitate the search for food.

PLATE I

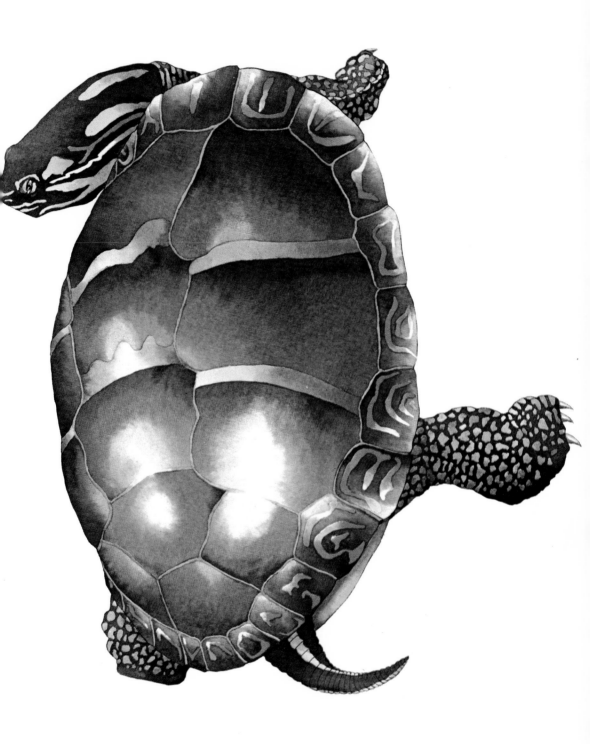

Red-Eared Turtle

Chrysemys scripta elegans

The red-eared turtle, a subspecies of the pond slider, is an inhabitant of the Mississippi Valley, from Illinois to the Gulf of Mexico. During courtship, the male red-eared carefully vibrates his foreclaws against the neck and head of a female. When the sale of baby turtles was still legal, the red-eared was among the most popular in the pet trade. Red-eared turtles are still collected for research. Thousands are destroyed when they leave the water and attempt to cross highways in their overland travels. This subspecies, like all the pond slider subspecies, is in trouble.

PLATE II

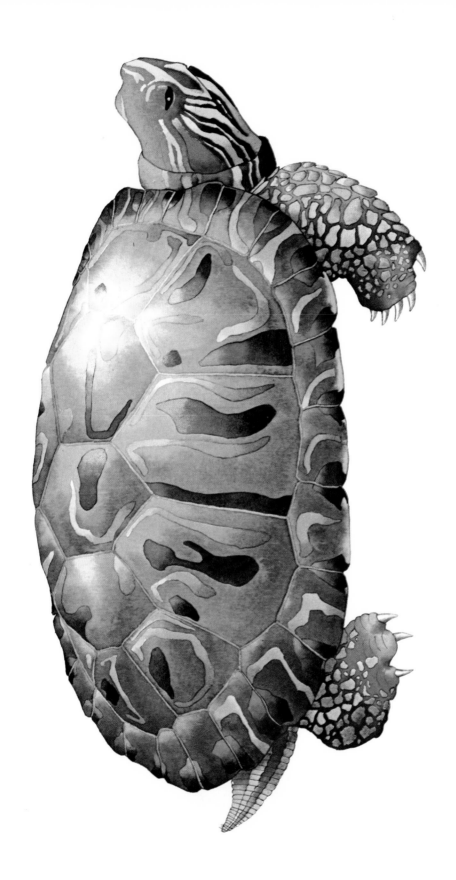

Florida Box Turtle

Terrapene carolina bauri

This subspecies of box turtle is restricted to the Florida peninsula and the Keys. It is distinguished by a carapace featuring a pattern of bright, radiating lines. The Florida box turtle differs from the other subspecies only in the manner of sexual intercourse. The male, pulsating his yellow throat, gently woos the female and, after climbing onto her carapace, nips softly at her neck.

PLATE III

Northern Diamondback Terrapin

Malaclemys terrapin terrapin

The diamondback terrapin is the only species of North American turtle to inhabit the salt marshes of the eastern coastline. It is largely carnivorous, taking crabs, clams, snails, and insects. Active throughout the day, the diamondback spends much of its time either basking or prowling through coves, lagoons, tidal flats, and estuaries. Because of its savory flesh, the diamondback was heavily collected throughout its range. Once seriously depleted, the species is beginning to stage a comeback in some areas.

PLATE IV

Yellow-Bellied Turtle

Chrysemys scripta scripta

The yellow-bellied turtle is a subspecies of the pond slider. It is aquatic, with a preference for bodies of quiet water having soft bottoms and thick growths of aquatic vegetation. While juveniles are primarily carnivorous, adults eat large amounts of vegetable matter. Until the sale of baby turtles was banned by the federal government, the yellow-bellied turtle and the other subspecies of the pond slider were the most popular species in the pet turtle trade.

PLATE V

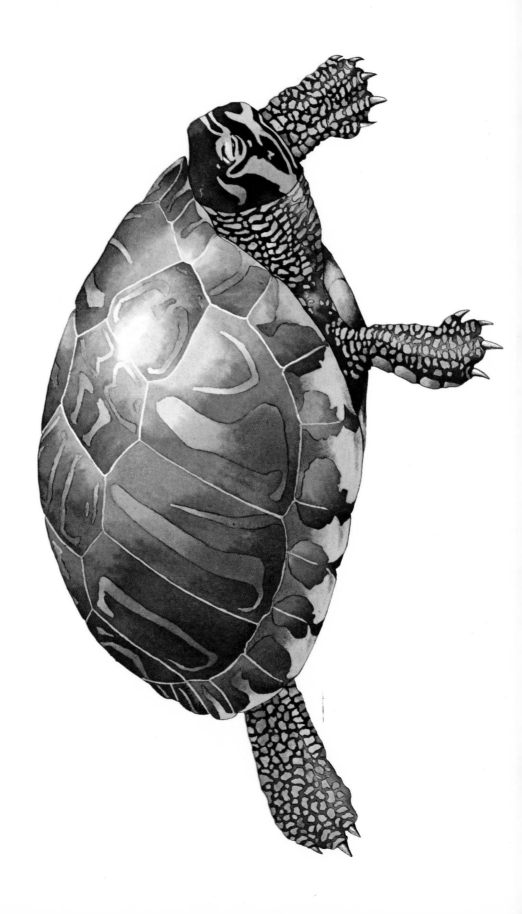

Yellow Mud Turtle

Kinosternon flavescens flavescens

The yellow mud turtle is a small aquatic species found in almost any kind of body of fresh water, including rivers, lakes, streams, ponds, swamps, sloughs, sinkholes, and even cattle troughs. It prefers an area having an oozy bottom and abundant aquatic vegetation. The yellow mud turtle also spends time on land, searching for food, basking, or traveling between bodies of water. Its life history is incompletely known.

PLATE VI

Wood Turtle

Clemmys insculpta

The wood turtle is one of the handsomest of North American turtles. Its carapace has a sculptured appearance that is both striking and unique. It is terrestrial, found in woods, bogs, marshes, and pastures. Omnivorous and active throughout the day, the wood turtle is fond of basking and proficient at climbing. It has the reputation of being one of the smartest of turtles, with individuals exhibiting definite personalities.

PLATE VII

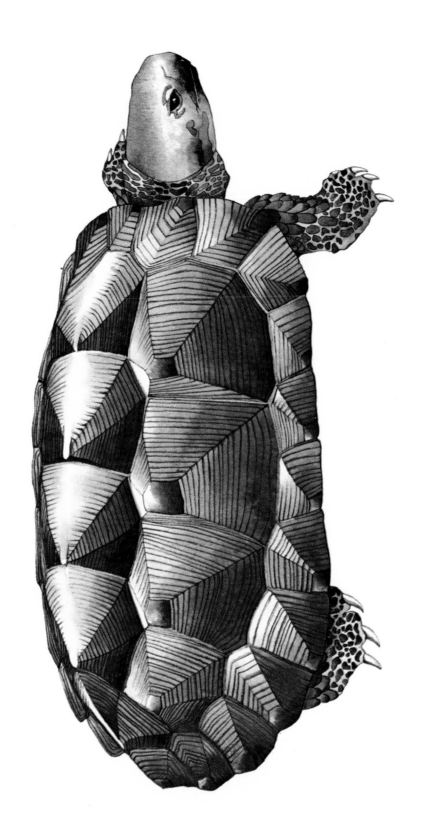

Eastern Mud Turtle

Kinosternon subrubrum subrubrum

The eastern mud turtle is a small species found in bodies of fresh water. It prefers shallow water having areas with soft bottoms and plentiful aquatic vegetation. This omnivorous chelonian spends much of the day prowling the bottom for food. It also frequently leaves the water to wander about on land.

PLATE VIII

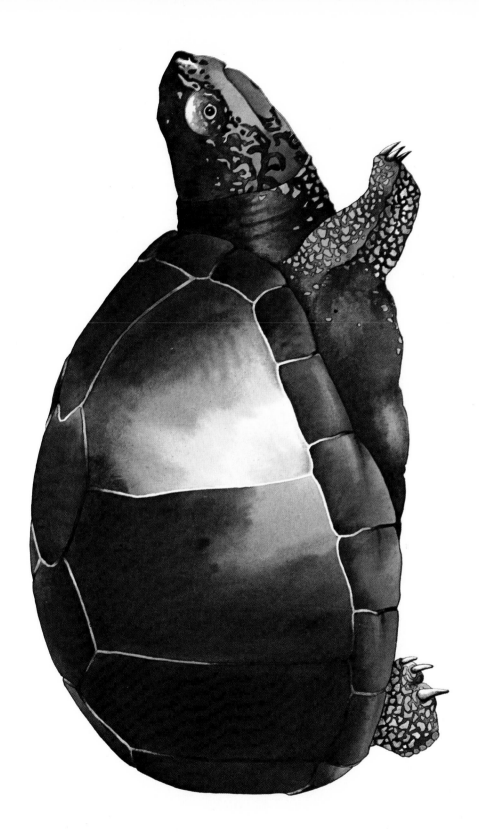

Southern Painted Turtle

Chrysemys picta dorsalis

A small aquatic turtle, the southern painted is one of the four subspecies of the painted turtle. Territorially, the four subspecies taken together span the continent—the only chelonian species to do so. All painted turtles prefer slow currents and shallow water, such as lakes, creeks, ponds, and marshes. They are omnivorous, taking whatever small aquatic animals or plants are available. Painted turtles are often locally abundant; sometimes they are eaten, and sometimes taken as pets.

PLATE IX

Map Turtle

Graptemys geographica

The map turtle is a medium-sized aquatic species, preferring spacious bodies of water, such as lakes, large ponds, or rivers. An area having a variety of basking sites, abundant aquatic vegetation, and a slow current is preferred. Very wary chelonians, map turtles spend much of the day basking and gathering together in crowds that may end up piled several deep on a log or rock. They are carnivorous, with a taste for snails, clams, insects, and crayfish. Because they consume large numbers of a species of snail harboring a parasite harmful to humans and other mammals, they are of benefit to humans.

PLATE X

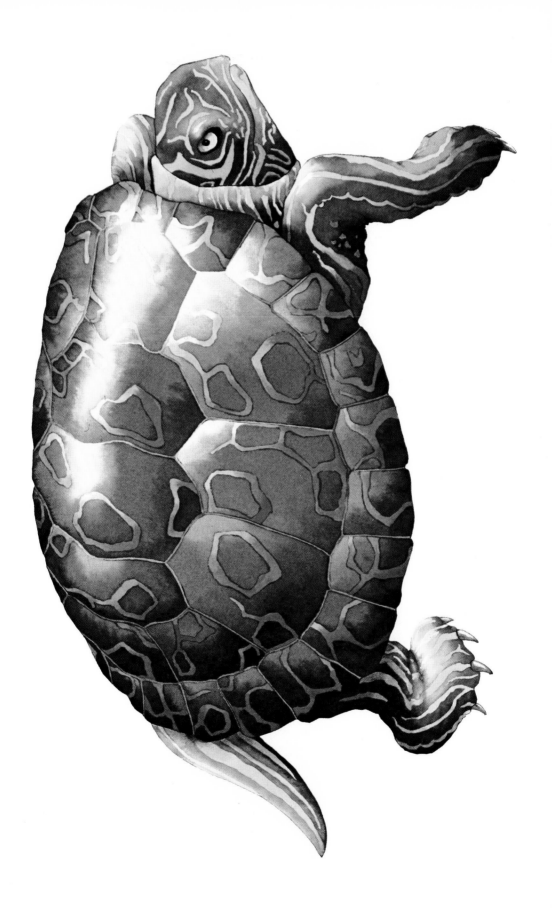

Alabama Map Turtle

Graptemys pulchra

The Alabama map is a smaller than average aquatic turtle, found in the Gulf coastal streams. It prefers deep bodies of water having slow currents and sandy bottoms. While it spends many hours basking during the day, this very wary chelonian cannot generally be approached closely. Primarily carnivorous, the Alabama map turtle is quite abundant in some parts of its range. Much of its life history is still unknown.

PLATE XI

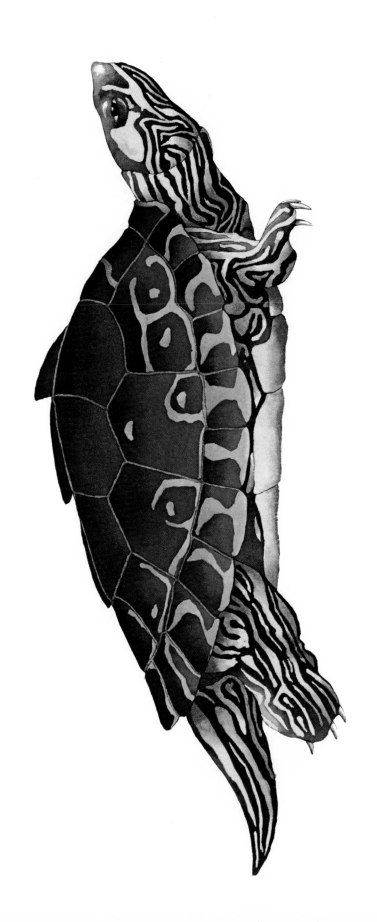

The Life Cycle of Turtles

Pictured on the previous two facing pages, the life cycle of turtles is condensed to illustrate the basic chelonian activities. Copulation, the excavation of a nest, and the laying of eggs are all part of producing new generations. Basking, and searching out food, are activities essential to maintaining the present generation. What cannot be so easily illustrated is the degree to which turtles—both aquatic and terrestrial—have adapted to their varying environments and formed an essential, healthy link with their complexly balanced habitats.

PLATE XII

Eastern Box Turtle

Terrapene carolina carolina

The four subspecies of box turtles found in North America are among the most familiar of all chelonians. Box turtles are small terrestrial creatures. The eastern box turtle is found in pastures, meadows, and woodlands having little undergrowth. All box turtles are omnivorous. They are mild by nature—a quality which, above all others, has caused them to become popular pets. In addition, they are among the most visible of turtles, as they do not take refuge in water.

PLATE XIII

PART II

Turtles and People

4

Exploitation by Homo Sapiens

The history of the interactions between turtles and humans can be divided into two basic activities. We have admired them, and sometimes even kept them as pets. Or we've eaten them—and made oil from their fats, and used their shells for containers and jewelry. The activities are not mutually exclusive. Still, eating turtle flesh is by far the more common practice. For a very long time humans have been consuming turtles with gusto, yet until very recently we have known very little about them. Many facets of their lives and their habits have been a mystery to us, a record sealed shut by our inability (or unwillingness) to read it. Or, perhaps, we have cared to learn only what we had to know in order to catch turtles: what characteristics differentiate them? where are they found? what is the best time of day to catch them? what is the most efficient method? These have been our primary concerns.

Here we are concerned with the taking of turtles for food and, to a lesser extent, with the exploitation of turtles for other purposes as well. Many valuable lessons about the plight of North American turtles are to be learned from the examples of certain Central and South American practices. Although little work has yet been done in the history of chelonian exploitation, what is known tells the outline of a tale that is largely grim: for the taking of turtles for food has often been not only uncontrolled, but reckless of any attempt at maintaining stable populations. Some species of turtles have been driven close to extinction by hunting. Others may already be too depleted to recover. And, to be sure, the generation of a few species now living will soon be the last.

Recent excavations in Ethiopia have unearthed skeletons of hominids, precursors of modern man, that have been established as being three million years old. The history of interactions between chelonians and these ancestral human forms probably dates back to at least that time. (See Comparative Chronology, p. 18.) Although the area in which the bones were found is now a dry and barren land, fossil evidence indicates that three million years ago it was lush, composed of grasslands, woodlands, and many rivers and streams. A long-extinct though impressively large species of tortoise, sporting a shell a yard wide, has been attributed to the now-Ethiopian portion of northeast Africa. Scientists investigating the site conjecture that turtle eggs would have made an excellent addition to the hominid diet—easy and safe to gather, and particularly rich in protein. Indeed, it is logical to assume that the predecessors of *Homo sapiens*, constantly engaged in a rough struggle to survive, should find in the abundant supplies of turtle eggs an excellent supplement to an unstable diet. In addition, small turtles may have been collected, if the hominid species in question then had tools capable of cracking a shell open. This point has not yet been resolved. Yet it can be said that turtles have unwittingly played a part, however humble, in the development of the hominids, that is, in the successful emergence of human beings.

It may be, over this three-million year span, that humans were responsible for eradicating local populations of turtles, and, perhaps, even endangering the survival of some species. We can be certain that humans included turtles as a regular part of their diets by 20,000 B.C., although, presumably, there is no reason to doubt that people (or proto-people) had ever stopped taking turtles or their eggs when the opportunity arose. The scanty evidence available indicates that turtles seem to have been eaten in just about every area in which their range and that of human territories overlapped.

The city states of Mesopotamia—the first urban centers to rise above the status of villages—were aware of turtles and tortoises native to their section of the Near East, as various images in clay and cuneiform writing indicate. Egypt, next to develop a complex civilization, was also well aware of turtles. They appear in inventories of wildlife and in murals. However, they may not have been taken for food, as the Egyptian religion identified turtles with death and the forces of evil. They were thus generally detested. Were they destroyed when found, I wonder, by the zealous, or were they allowed to pursue their own sinister ways? Elsewhere in Africa, Europe, and the Americas, both simple and very complex societies included turtles or tortoises as either common fare or an occasional addition to their diets.

Hunting in the Amazon

Numerous methods for taking turtles have evolved over the ages. Collecting groups of turtles by trapping them in nets, and individual turtles by spearing or shooting them with arrows, are the most common. Henry Walter Bates' superb work, *The Naturalist on the River Amazons* (London, 1863), describing his eleven years spent exploring the Amazon River Basin in the middle of the nineteenth century, includes very precise descriptions of the settlers' and natives' methods of collecting the then-abundant turtles of the region. With some allowance for small differences in technique, his descriptions provide an accurate image of turtle hunting as it was practiced anytime, anywhere, during the past thousands of years.

Bates first describes how the local Indians shot turtles with arrows. "I was astonished at the skill which the Indians display in shooting turtles. They did not wait for their coming to the surface to breathe, but watched for the slight movements in the water which revealed their presence underneath. . . . The instant one was perceived an arrow flew from the bow of the nearest man, and never failed to pierce the shell of the submerged animal.

"The arrow used in turtle shooting has a strong lancet-shaped steel point, fitted into a peg which enters the tip of the shaft. The peg is secured to the shaft by twine made of the fibres of pine-apple leaves, the twine being some thirty or forty yards in length, and neatly wound round the body of the arrow. When the missile enters the shell, the peg drops out, and the pierced animal descends with it towards the bottom, leaving the shaft floating on the surface. . . . The sportsman . . . gently draws the animal by the twine, humouring it by giving it the rein when it plunges, until it is brought again near the surface, when he strikes it with a second arrow. . . . He has then no difficulty in landing his game."

That afternoon, the Indians accompanying Bates spread out a net to close off a pool located close to the delta on which they traveled. While several Indians held the net in place, "The rest of the party then spread themselves around the swamp at the opposite end of the pool, and began to beat, with stout poles, the thick tufts of Matupá, in order to drive the turtles towards the middle. This was continued for an hour or more, the beaters gradually drawing nearer to each other, and driving the hosts of animals before them; the number of little snouts constantly popping above the surface of the water showing that all was going on well. When they neared the net, the men moved more quickly, shouting and beating with great vigour. The ends of the net were then seized by several strong hands and dragged suddenly forwards, bringing them at the same time together, so as to enclose all the booty in a circle. Every man now leapt into the inclosure, the boats were brought up, and the turtles easily captured by the hand and tossed into them."

Within twenty minutes about eighty turtles had been secured. Another eighty were soon added to the pile. According to Bates the turtles, which were between six to eighteen inches in length, supplied them with meat for several months. "Roasted in the shell they form a most appetizing dish." Bates goes on to observe that a similar drive was attempted the next day, but with disappointing results. The Indians told him that, although many turtles remained in the pool, they had learned by the previous day's experience not to respond. The sly ones survived.

Bates witnessed one last method of exploiting turtle populations: an egg hunt. The communal nesting ground of the turtles having been found, and the turtles having been observed to nest there in large numbers, sentries were posted to protect the area. The entire population of the nearest village was notified of the event. A census was taken, with the heads of each household being required to pay 140 reis (less than a half-dollar) for the right of their families to participate in the collection. After the village had assembled around the site, the signal to begin was given by a roll of drums. "It was an animating sight to behold the wide circle of rival diggers throwing up clouds of sand in their energetic labors, and working gradually towards the center of the ring. By the end of the second day . . . large mounds of eggs, some of them from four to five feet in height, were then seen by the side of each hut, the produce of the labours of the family."

A family could take as much as they could dig out. "The destruction of turtle eggs every year by these proceedings is enormous." The principal use of the eggs was the oil that could be extracted from them and used for a variety of purposes or sold at a profit. Knowing how many eggs were needed for one jar of oil, and having found out how many jars of oil were reported that year, Bates estimated that, in the Upper Amazon Basin, the "total number of eggs annually destroyed amounts . . . to 48,000,000." It should come as no surprise, then, that species of turtles commonly found in the Amazon have, since the mid-nineteenth century, greatly declined.

While the episodes Bates describes are on a far larger scale than most, they do accurately indicate the attitudes humans have often held towards turtles and the methods used to collect them. However, it would be useless to condemn such behavior out of hand. Turtles and humans are linked in the fragile web of existence. Turtle eggs and turtle flesh have often been an important source of protein for people who are too poor to obtain it in any other way or who live in a location where few other dependable sources of protein are available. It would be insensitive, and mistaken, to dismiss such peoples out of hand as wanton destroyers of nature. Their objective is to survive, to maintain themselves and their families in a way of life where starvation or malnutrition has often been the norm. That they have shown little concern for, or little understanding of, the species they search out and kill is not exceptional. We, who have the benefit of greater knowledge and a wider view of the fabrics of nature have not often done much better. Even had they understood some of the dangers of relying too heavily on a species, it is unlikely that they would have been able much to alter their behavior. Today, it is impossible for some groups to be ecologically mindful, as they and the turtles they seek have become entangled in a complex net of economic circumstances.

The Miskito: A Cautionary Tale

The Miskito people of Central America provide an extreme example of the difficulties—because of economic and political entanglements—in acknowledging a severe ecological problem and implementing conservation techniques to deal with it.

In a time now past, the men would rise long before the dawn and haul their canoes down to the ocean's edge. Food, containers of water, ropes, paddles, sails, and harpoons would be carefully distributed, balanced, and secured throughout the twenty-foot boats so that nothing would be swept over the low sides of the craft. Pushing the canoes into the water, two men would climb into each. In the bow one would stand and, using a long pole, drive the canoe through the surf. The other would kneel in the stern and with a paddle of mahogany taller than a man keep the boat on a straight course.

Once outside the waves of the shoreline, they rig their sail and set their course by a star bright in the eastern sky. Soon after dawn they will reach the point already agreed upon, having been carried to it by the winds and the shrewd reckoning of the "captain" in the stern. It is a spot they have visited before.

In the unbroken expanses of water they paddle. Each motion is as careful and as quiet as it can be made. What they wait for is the sound of a powerful, prolonged hiss, as if the very water were cracked by intense pressure. When the sound is heard, the men are ready to act. Without consulting, with only the briefest moment to center in on the position of the noise, they push with urgency towards the source. The "strikerman" in the bow has his harpoon close by. It is made of a wooden shaft, eight to ten feet in length, with a detachable barb, and with a long, strong line fixed to it; he wields a harpoon whose design has been perfected over centuries of use. What the captain and strikerman are looking for is the great broad back of a surfaced green turtle.

The turtle is known to interrupt its browsing through the thick fields of aquatic vegetation below and come up to draw in air; expelling its used air produces the loud hiss. The canoe must be driven directly behind or before the turtle. Quickly, on a rocking boat, with little time to sight, the man in the bow must with great force cast his harpoon at the target. Once struck, the turtle will respond instinctively. Submerging, driving itself forward to escape the great pain that has cracked it open, pounding along until it becomes exhausted, it must finally surface. The men must be prepared for this desperate, convulsive act. They must maintain their balance in the boat, retrieve the shaft of the harpoon, and feed out the line. When they sense the diminished energy at the other end, the turtle is hauled in. They pierce its flippers, thread strong cord through the holes, and tie them down. The turtle is turned and laid on its back in the canoe, immobilized, dying in a stolid silence punctuated occasionally by gasps.

The men will go on hunting. For they know that the green turtles have always fed on certain great fields of subterranean vegetation—and the location of these fields, and of the shoals where the turtles congregate to spend the night, have been plotted and re-plotted for centuries. Where there is one turtle, there will be more.

When the boat is full, or the day through, the men will set their sails to catch the northeast trade wind. And thus they are carried home.

Word rapidly spreads of the men's return. Relatives and friends gather to haul the loaded canoes over the beach and into the sheds where they are stored. There the turtles are butchered; meat and other products are distributed to relatives and friends of the fishermen. In this way the great skill of the few are placed at the disposal of an entire village. All receive necessary protein, and—in the ritualistic distribution of the flesh—all participate in a renewal of social bonds. The turtles now belong to all, for their hunters and their success have become the vehicle by which a communal interdependence is renewed.

The people call themselves the Miskito. Before any white men, before even Columbus had fallen upon the Caribbean, they had settled in that land where they are *still* to be found, the eastern shore of Nicaragua. Because of a special dedication to the pursuit of turtles and their real affinity for oceanic navigation, or perhaps simply because of historical accident, the Miskito came to be among the very best hunters of turtles in the entire Caribbean. But hunting turtles was only one aspect of their existence, one activity of a varied routine for survival. They also fished, hunted game in the jungles beyond their villages, and practiced a form of subsistence farming. In this manner, the Miskito generally had enough. Because they subsisted on various sources, they placed no exceptional strain on any particular one of them. They took what they needed, and no more than that: there was no reason to be excessive—so long as they minded only themselves.

But the advent of Europeans to the Caribbean waters provided a reason. The foreign conquerors needed meat and were willing to pay for it, at first with trade goods, later with money. In a sense, the abundant, cheap supply of turtle meat made the success of the Europeans possible. It fed them, and then it fed the workers attracted to the great agricultural estates, to the mines, and to the logging industry. As more and more of the native inhabitants were drawn to the cities, they too became dependent on an imported supply of protein, being unable to obtain it for themselves. Dazzled by the goods now available to them, the Miskito (and other groups) soon fell victim to the new system. They abandoned the old, balanced ways, either enlisting in the industries or supplying meat for the workers. They stopped farming, hunting, and fishing—except for those catches, such as turtles, which could bring in a profit.

The industries, based on intensive short-term exploitation, began one-by-one to shut down as the supplies of raw materials ran out. People such as the Miskito, now dependent on their earned money to purchase food, were further buffeted by the changes. Having ceased to collect their own food in the wild, or even to do more than intermittent farming, they were entrenched in a cash economy. The only thing they had left to sell, when the labor market disappeared, was the turtle: its flesh, skin, shell, oil, and calipee (the edible, fatty, gelatinous substance attached to the plastron). They concentrated on the turtle, going out now for days, even for weeks at a time, to hunt them. It was no longer sufficient to take what one needed. One had to take as many turtles as could be found and loaded on a canoe. In the late 1960s two factories funded by foreign firms were built along the Nicaraguan coast to process quantities of turtle meat and products for sale abroad. Located close to the Miskito villages, they enabled the fishermen to stay out for even longer periods of time, as it was no longer necessary to transport the turtles any distance. The turtle companies encourage the Miskito to stay out for long periods of time by giving them materials to build shelters on distant cays.

Company boats make a weekly stop at such camps, paying for turtles on hand, dropping off food or other materials. As the men are away from their homes for longer and longer periods of time, new pressures are placed on family and village life.

Taking turtles by harpooning them, as was their custom, is a lengthy and demanding process that would yield only a few turtles in a day. Necessarily, their old skills have been abandoned. Now the Miskitos go out armed with fifty-foot-long nets. Suspended like great walls, the nets stand vertically beneath the surface. They are dropped in place near the known nocturnal resting sites of the green turtles. During the night, the turtles will periodically surface for air; by so doing they risk becoming ensnared in the nets. Literally thousands of nets are set each day. All that is required of the turtle hunters are daily trips to collect the helpless catch.

In a bitter irony, the more turtles the Miskito take, the less protein they are getting. As they must now buy their food from local stores, they need cash. They can only get cash by selling turtles. They cannot afford to save much meat for themselves. Flour, beans, rice, sugar, and coffee are the new staples of the Miskito diet. Such a diet lacks protein; it is, compared to the diet of their ancestors, plain, limited, and enfeebling. The necessity of selling turtles has had a final, devastating effect. The flesh can no longer be shared out with relatives and friends. Bitterness, suspicion, and the collapse of traditional group identity are the results. Now each man is on his own. The old ritual dies, and with it the communal identity of the Miskito, the consciousness of shared responsibility and shared life.

Such a situation would be desperate enough. Soon, however, conditions are likely to be intolerable. Subjected to a hundred years of relentless exploitation, green turtles are now beginning to disappear at an ever accelerating rate. Miskito hunters must stay out for longer and longer periods to find them; and when they do come home, they come with fewer turtles than formerly. Within several years, it is likely that there will be too few turtles, too widely scattered, to make hunting them worthwhile. What will the Miskito do then? Incapable or unwilling to turn back to the old subsistence economy (based on hunting, fishing, and farming), compelled to survive in an economic system depending on cash (which they can no longer get), they can look forward to an existence only more difficult—even wretched. Perhaps if their villages regained some image of cohesion and communality, the people could collectively find a way to meet the problem and reinstate their sense of unique identity. But the very industry that has supported them has encouraged the collapse of collective responsibility and altruistic behavior. When the turtle goes, what can the Miskito do?

The Uses of the Sea Turtle

Peoples in the Caribbean and elsewhere in the world are as dependent on other species of sea-going chelonians as are the Miskito on green turtles. Indeed, all species of sea turtle are hunted, some for their meat, others for their shells, yet others for their oils. While the green turtle is probably the most frequent victim, unrestricted exploitation now has reduced all the sea turtles to terribly small populations. All of the marine species occur in the waters, or nest on the beaches, of many countries—their diffusion makes any effort toward conservation problematic. Any policy of conservation, to be effective, will have to be coordinated and rigorously applied throughout the wide range of the turtles. But most of the countries in whose waters these turtles dwell are poor; they lack the money, the manpower—and often the will—to patrol the waters and beaches against poachers.

Many of these countries have suffered from both chronically high unemployment levels and severe shortages of cheap protein, resulting in malnutrition. In such lands, the turtles are both a vital part of the people's diet and an important factor in the country's economy. To outlaw the collection of sea turtles, if it were possible, would cause great immediate hardship, and undoubtedly a flourishing black market. However, if some effort at conservation is not agreed upon, the turtles will soon be altogether gone, or reduced to such low populations that no turtle industry could survive. The troubles now afflicting the Miskito may be a portent of things to come.

Unlike the green turtle, hunted mostly for its flesh, the hawksbill turtle is sought for its shell—the exquisite tortoiseshell that has long been a prized possession in many parts of the world. Winning the shell of *Eretmochelys imbricata* nowadays is routine. Most often the turtle is killed, the outer layer of the shell peeled off, and the corpse thrown overboard. However, this was not always the case. E. G. Squires, American ambassador to Nicaragua, described in 1855 the process by which the shell was peeled from living turtles:

> When the turtle is caught they fasten him, and cover his back with dry leaves or grass, to which they set fire. The heat causes the plates to separate at the joint. A large knife is then inserted horizontally beneath them, and the laminae lifted from the back, care being taken not to injure the shell by too much heat, nor to force it off, until the heat has fully prepared it for separation. Many turtles die under this cruel operation, but instances are numerous in which they have been caught a second time, with the outer coating reproduced; but in these cases, instead of thirteen pieces, it is a single piece. As I have already said, I could never bring myself to witness this cruelty more than once, and was glad that the process of "scaling" was carried on out of sight. . . . Had the poor turtles the power of shrieking, they would have made that barren island a very hell, with their cries of torture.

A single hawksbill can yield up to twelve pounds of tortoiseshell. The product, translucent, streaked with swirls of red, white, brown, green, and black, has not diminished in popularity, even with the advent of man-made substitutes. So far, efforts at conservation have been largely unavailing. And among many of those whose job it is to take the hawksbill, the work is the best that they can find in areas in which unemloyment is chronic. The individuals that benefit most from the tortoiseshell industry are the wholesalers, and among them greed far outweighs any concern for the species. When the hawksbill goes down for good, they will be best able to take their profits and move on to other projects. Unless something is done, the hawksbill certainly will soon disappear.

The loggerhead, *Caretta caretta,* is one of the few marine species which the United States can have any direct influence in preserving. Its nesting sites along the eastern coast have continued to dwindle as developers chew up once pristine beaches and islands for home sites and recreational facilities. By identifying the sites favored by the loggerheads, and by extending them protection from development, it *may* be possible to preserve the Atlantic subspecies of *Caretta caretta.* Yes, as the loggerhead continues to be taken throughout the world for its flesh and eggs, the possible disappearance of the entire North American breeding population can only further contribute to the failure of the species.

At present, in the slow but steady race that marine turtles are running toward extinction, the Atlantic ridley is outdistancing the other species. Until well into the twentieth century, the major nesting site of *Lepidochelys kempii* along the Gulf Coast of Mexico (in fact, the one remaining major nesting site of the ridley) was unknown. But when it was finally located, it was immediately, disastrously, pillaged. The collection of eggs and the slaughter of nesting females during the first several years after the discovery were so thorough that it is doubtful whether more than a few score ridleys hatched and made it into the sea. This egg-plundering sort of exploitation, in addition to the hunting of adult turtles for meat, soon decimated the number of ridleys. Although Mexican soldiers armed with submachine guns now patrol the few strips of beach still used by the ridleys during the nesting season, it is questionable whether the species can make a comeback.

The Pacific ridley *(Lepidochelys olivacea)* may be in somewhat better shape. For it is less frequently hunted, and several of its nesting beaches— too isolated to be developed for use by men—have not yet been exploited by egg-hunters.

While the worldwide population of the leatherback turtle is not large, with as few as 1000 females capable of nesting, there was until recently no immediate danger of extinction. *Dermochelys coriacea* has no shell, is inedible, and yields no usable fat. However, the situation may be changing: the base of some cosmetics now in use is derived from the oils of this turtle. If the leatherback suddenly becomes lucrative, there will be many willing to exploit it. Such a small population could not long survive any severe pressure. There are other equivalent oils for use as a cosmetic base, *all* of them synthetic. As with many products derived from whales, there are alternatives, would the manufacturers only turn to them.

North American Fare: Diamondbacks and Snappers

Presumably, the colonists learned from the original inhabitants of America, who had been catching and eating turtles for thousands of years, which species were worth consuming. That the Indians ate turtles and tortoises, and that the explorers and colonists were not slow to catch on, is indicated by this observation from Thomas Hariot's *Brief and True Report of the New Found Land of Virginia:* "Tortoises, both of the land and sea varieties, are more than a yard in breadth, with thick shells on their backs and bellies. Their heads, feet and tails look very ugly, like those of a venomous serpent. Nevertheless, they are very good to eat, as are their eggs." Hariot's book was published in London in 1588.

During the past three hundred years North Americans have added several native chelonian species to their diets. But because many North American turtle species occur in fairly limited areas, their use as food has been restricted to specific regions of the continent. Only two species, owing to their large numbers, wide ranges, and particularly succulent flesh, have won wide culinary favor: diamondbacks and snappers, having thus transcended merely regional popularity, sustain a gastronomic popularity that has had no inconsiderable effect on them.

Found at one time all along the eastern coastline from Cape Cod to Florida, the marsh-dwelling diamondback turtle is the unfortunate possessor of a succulent, fleshy body. It must have been one of the first species of turtles that the seventeenth-century colonists encountered. And if they were at all slow in realizing what an excellent addition the diamondback made to their often skimpy fare, they could certainly have followed the example of their near natives, the inaccurately named "Indians" of North America, who regularly roasted *Malaclemys terrapin.*

At first, the diamondback existed in such great numbers that it was treated as an unexceptional and easily obtained addition to the diet. It was far easier to obtain than, say, a deer. Indeed, familiarity may have bred dissatisfaction. In Tidewater, Virginia, diamondbacks were considered the cheapest source of protein for the numbers of slaves held on the great plantations. History records at one point a prolonged protest mounted by the slaves over their unvarying diet of turtle meat.

That styles in eating may alter widely over time, and for no logical reason, is indicated by the fate of the diamondback. By the end of the nineteenth century it had become one of the most prized additions to the meals of the upper classes. The most discriminating hotels and restaurants served it, suitably gotten up with sauces and imaginative titles. When the elite of the "Golden Nineties" sat down to a fifteen- or sixteen-course meal, diamondback would likely be on the bill of fare. Those intent on copying the whims and lifestyle of the elite naturally favored it. The fad for diamondbacks reached its peak in the first decade of the twentieth century, when a single specimen could fetch as much as ten dollars on the market, and a dozen adult turtles could cost anywhere from 90 to 120 dollars. Just *why* this complete shift in attitude should have taken place is a mystery. Perhaps it occurred because a promoter (either shrewd or desperate) saw a chance to introduce diamondback to a market always anxious for culinary novelties. Turtles were abundant, cost little to obtain, and could be shipped still living to market, thus ensuring fresh merchandise.

However, the population remaining in the marshes at the end of the nineteenth century was not large enough to long sustain intensive harvesting. To meet the ever increasing demand, commercial "farms" were established to churn out diamondbacks in a factory-like manner. Whereas little study has been done on the diamondback in its native environment, there is a mountainous pile of available information on raising the species in captivity, and on maximizing the quantity and the tenderness of the flesh of the product.

Just as there is no explanation for the sudden elevation of the diamondback to gourmet status, there is no way to explain its sudden decline in favor. Perhaps the farms proved uneconomical. In many areas the populations of diamondbacks in the wild had been eliminated, cleaned out in the scrabble for cash. The diminishing supply may have discouraged sales and caused suppliers to turn to other, more readily available foods. One example should serve to indicate the effect of unrestricted harvesting on the species. In 1891, 90,000 pounds of diamondback were collected in Chesapeake Bay. In 1920, the most diligent efforts were needed to bring in 800 pounds.

The diamondback has not yet recovered from this long binge of popularity. While it has begun to repopulate some of the areas from which it was eradicated, large parts of its former marshy territory are still empty of it. In some of the areas in which the diamondback has managed to hang on, it has done so in such small numbers that a single serious catastrophe (an oil spill, the release of chemical wastes, even a very harsh winter) would be enough to push it toward extinction. Two hundred years of steady collection, and thirty years of unrestricted, unsupervised, thoughtless exploitation have reduced a once very common animal to the status of a rare, endangered species.

Snappers, too, have pleased many a palate, but with their reputation for tasty flesh, North American snapping turtles are the only chelonians to have a widespread reputation for consistently aggressive behavior. Yet their behavior has not deterred hunters intent on collecting them for the pot. Indeed, the snappers' bristly behavior may even have provided an excuse, were one needed, for taking them and making of them a savory dish. (In the same way, though a much more extreme case, no one sheds tears for the piranha—that voracious carnivorous fish found in South America, collected in great numbers by many tribes living along the rivers, fished out and thrown upon banks to gasp out its life.)

Snappers were taken by native Americans for centuries before the land was claimed by colonists. And soon after the land was colonized, the settlers added the snapper to their diets. While not quite so popular as it once was, the snapper is still a well-known dish in some regions. Indeed, in the city in which I work, snapper soup has long been a local favorite. Every week, some 500 pounds of snapper are brought in, to be rendered into soup for local use and for distribution elsewhere.

It might be tempting to ascribe the snapper's temperament to the fact that the turtle is so heavily collected for food. But, having established their behavior patterns millions of years ago, they manifest a distinct departure from the traditional chelonian mode. Turtles have evolved by mastering the arts of strategic retreat. Indeed, by the process of evolution the turtle has turned into a kind of portable cave, capable of withdrawing into itself, into a safe, bony refuge when trouble threatens. Snappers use disguise, as do all turtles, as the first, most important level of defense: if you aren't seen, you can't be threatened. But, once threatened, snappers distinguish themselves from most other turtles by going on the offense, by striking out. This aggressive instinct is as firmly encoded in them as is the meekness engrained in some other species of turtles. Snappers begin their threat displays, opening wide their jaws and snapping them shut, as soon as they emerge from the egg. The loud and impressive display explains how the snappers got their common name. It is probably the first feature of the turtle to impress itself on someone confronting a snapper out of water for the first time.

However, snappers are *not* alone in this reaction. Other species of turtle may also react to danger by attacking. Snappers simply seem to attack more frequently and to carry through an assault with greater vigor. There is a folk saying claiming that a snapper will not let go of a person "until the sun goes down or thunder rolls." This is a great exaggeration, but I'm certain the idea behind it—the snapper's great tenacity in maintaining a hold—is based on painful first-hand experience.

Why is the snapper so aggressive? Possibly because it is more vulnerable to attack than other turtles: its shell is greatly reduced. Its plastron is so small as to seem a mere afterthought, a symbolic gesture. There is a lot of flesh for any sharp-toothed predator to take a hold on. In addition, the snapper is a predator itself. To live, it must be both fast and fatal in its attacks. Further, the snapper is an aquatic turtle. When it ventures on land, it is out of its element and is especially touchy about being threatened. If disturbed in its native element, the snapper has the choice to move quickly away or to disappear into mud or underwater vegetation; and it will generally exercise such an option. On land, separated from its refuge, it will fight to survive. There is nothing in its behavior that can be understood as being malignant, as indicating a planned searching out and harrying of humans. It is just trying to strike some bargain with survival. While people do get bitten by snappers submerged in the water, I think the majority of these cases are caused by mistaken identity (when the snapper, seeing only a part of a human, mistakes it for something edible), or by a misreading of the human's presence as an indication of a distinct threat. If you come too close to a snapper's underwater hideout, it may react as if it were being pursued.

There are three species of snapper. The alligator snapper (*Macroclemys temminckii*) and the common snapper (*Chelydra serpentina*) are regularly taken. The Florida snapper (*Chelydra osceola*) generally is not. It has the most restricted range of the three and, as Archie Carr has suggested, may be generally ignored because within its territory there are other equally tasty or tastier species of turtles, including the softshells and the aptly named "Suwanee chicken," which is renowned locally for its tender, tasty flesh.

While many other species of North American turtles have been taken, or are still taken, for food, none has ever been so widely exploited as the snapper. There is a good reason for this: no other turtle covers such a wide territory. The common snapper can be found from southern Canada southward to the Gulf Coast, and from the Rocky Mountains eastward to the Atlantic Ocean. It has been found at elevations of up to 6000 feet. It has adapted to greatly varied conditions and, although no longer as common, as ubiquitous, as it once was, it does not seem to be endangered. It is certainly in better shape than the diamondback, the only other turtle collected over a very wide territory.

While snappers would be taken whether or not they exhibited aggressive tendencies, the fact that they have acquired a reputation for various sorts of nastiness makes killing them that much easier. Few voices have been raised on behalf of the discredited snapper, for who is willing to defend a creature both dangerous and tasty? Their reputed disposition has encouraged the idea that snappers *deserve* to be killed and eaten—on principle. Witness the image of the snapper given in Ernest Thompson Seton's *Rolf in the Woods* (1911):

> The boy's heart beat fast as he watched the bold swimmer and the savage reptile. There could be little doubt that the creature weighed a hundred pounds. It is the strongest for its size and the fiercest of all reptiles. Its jaws, though toothless, have cutting edges, a sharp beak, and power to the crushing of bones. Its armour makes it invulnerable to birds and beasts of prey. Like a log it lay on the beach, with its long alligator tail stretched up the banks and its serpentine head and tiny wicked eyes vigilantly watching the shore. Its shell, broad and ancient, was fringed with green moss, and its scaly armpits exposed, were decked with leeches. . . . Its huge limbs and claws were in marked conrast to the small, red eyes. But the latter it was that gave the thrill of unnervement.

The snapper in question is a great, vicious beast, dwelling in a pond close to the home of a sagacious Indian, Quonab, who in turn is introducing Rolf, an adolescent white, to the ways of the woods. Once a very popular novel, *Rolf* is an episodic record of the boy's development into a skilled woodsman. In one of the book's most exciting incidents, Quonab goes after the snapper—a behemoth that eats waterfowl, fouls the Indians' fishing lines, and cunningly escapes capture. As if such behavior isn't sufficient to condemn him, the snapper also stands accused of devouring Quonab's dog. After a vicious battle, the snapper is vanquished. Even after its head is severed from its body, the tremendous jaws keep on snapping, and the malevolent eyes gleam wickedly on. Quite exciting—but also inaccurate. Snappers, as we have noted, may be very aggressive on land; but in the water, where the climactic battle takes place, they are generally as reticent as any other species of turtle. Disturbed, they usually withdraw. Not one shred of evidence gathered in the field indicates a malignant attitude towards humanity.

Technology Versus Turtles

If the impact of North Americans on native turtles had been restricted just to matters of the stomach, matters would be serious enough. However, other factors have entered into the interactions between men and turtles, and today these factors pose a far greater challenge to the survival of some chelonian species.

While turtles continued to be taken for food, the gravest problems now facing North American chelonians include our destruction of their habitats, our pollution of the continent's fresh waters, and our cavalier attitude toward small creatures that get in our way. Nowhere is this attitude better exemplified than in the slaughter of turtles on our highways. By far, the greatest number of turtles dying from other than natural causes die as victims of the automobile. Even the most aquatic species are vulnerable to incidents of hit-and-run, for every species must come ashore to nest, and many must cross at least one road to reach a suitable nesting ground. Among the terrestrial species, however, the slaughter is most devastating. It is especially sad that so many of these deaths could be easily avoided if drivers took the effort to steer around turtles or even stop and carry the turtle to the side of the road it wishes to reach. (Never carry a turtle back to the side of the road from which it has come, for it will only insist on trying once again to cross the road.)

There are, admittedly, some individuals who take a special, warped delight in running down whatever turtles they come across. Such wretches, however, are in the minority. Driving more carefully, in a more alert manner, would certainly greatly reduce this toll in turtles. In the state in which I live there remains a small but apparently hardy group of diamondbacks. Every year, the females emerge from their marshy home, following much the same route through yards and over a well-traveled road to reach the nesting site. At one time, the number of females killed by cars was appallingly high. Very few made it to the area used year after year for nesting, and thus fewer and fewer diamondbacks were born. The hatchlings fared poorly as well, for they had to cross the road in order to reach the relative safety of the marshes. If this annual destruction had gone on much longer, I doubt whether the population of diamondbacks could have sustained itself. Fortunately, a group of local residents, appalled by the destruction, organized roadside patrols. As soon as the females emerged from the marshes (which they did, in numbers, within the space of a few days), the patrols would be called out, station themselves on either side of the road, and manage traffic while carrying the gravid females across. Once the females had laid their eggs and begun their return journey, the volunteers would once again turn out and carry the females across in the opposite direction. This process would be repeated for the hatchlings when they emerged from their eggs to seek out their native marsh. The local government encouraged the action, instructed the police to help, and even posted a roadside sign reading, "Slow, Turtle Crossing." The people involved were not, to my knowledge, particularly interested in *all* turtles, or even very adamant about the issue of conservation. What they knew about, and cared deeply about, were *their* turtles. They wanted to save a familiar and pleasing feature of their region, and they took steps to do so in a practical, direct manner. If such groups willing to give just a little time to the problem existed in towns across the country, the widespread destruction of turtles on the highways could be greatly reduced.

More generally, turtles suffer as much as (or more than) we do from dislocation, pollution, and poisons. We are forever draining marshes, filling in swamps, hewing down woodlands, laying down highways across fragile ecosystems, tearing out, filling in, pawing over, killing off. When land is torn out of its natural state, and fitted to our purposes, local populations of a variety of small animals are wiped out. They have, very often, no place to go, as more and more frequently untouched land exists as islands, surrounded on all sides by roads, homes, and factories. There are no corridors for escape.

The pollution of fresh-water habitats from industrial by-products has driven aquatic turtles from many areas they once inhabited. As yet unproved, but certainly within the realm of probability, is the deadly effect herbicides and insecticides may be having on turtles. Many kinds of poisons are carried from the land on which they have been applied into the fresh-water system to kill weeds or destructive insects. Very small aquatic creatures of various sorts are capable of absorbing quantities of the stuff; when these animals are in turn consumed by turtles, the poisons are consumed as well and may build up in dangerously high amounts in the fat of the fresh-water turtles. Terrestrial turtles come into direct contact with such poisons when they tramp across ground that has been treated, or when they eat small creatures that have ingested poisons—and there is, in many places, a virtual cornucopia of poisons coating the soil, the plants, and the trees.

In a sense, turtles provide an early warning system of the troubles we are visiting upon ourselves. As they now suffer from the degradation of the land and waters, so will we eventually suffer as the devastated land ceases to produce, as the life forms we depend upon die out of the waters. Thus, in taking steps to protect turtles, we are acting for our own good as well. By cleaning up the waters, reducing the numbers of poisons we use, and integrating land in a natural state into our designs, rather than simply bulldozing it away, we are acting to save ourselves as well as the wildlife of our continent. For in an area where turtles can flourish, so can many other species, including humans. The blueprint for conservation is thus cyclic in nature: in saving ourselves from the accelerating disruptions of careless growth and the careless usage of materials, we may save the turtles as well.

The Galapagos Tortoise

No species of turtle has suffered more grievously from the actions of men than has the giant land tortoise of the Galapagos Islands. While several species of sea turtles are approaching extinction, none is so perilously close to disappearing as these giant tortoises. Indeed, several subspecies of the Galapagos chelonians have already become extinct, victims of an unprincipled slaughter, a binge of destruction that has extended over some four hundred years. The interaction between man and tortoise has been, until quite recently, an unrelieved catastrophe for these unique creatures. In a bitter irony, repeated again and again in other parts of the world, the very qualities that contribute to the success of a species can, under altered circumstances, become deadly traps.

The Galapagos tortoises, *Geochelone elephantophus,* evolved in a location unknown to men, unvisited for millenia. The islands, located some six hundred miles from the western coast of South America, in a portion of the Pacific Ocean rarely traveled by ships, have few qualities to attract travelers, and fewer to keep them. The islands were for a long time known as the Encantadas, or Enchanted Isles, because of their reputed ability for shifting position. While the score of islands are not barren, they are rather bleak, and this bleakness, this utter isolation, also contributes to the air of mystery that has surfaced in many of the early descriptions of the Galapagos. If such qualities were not sufficient to earn for the place the title of "enchanted," certainly the appearance and behavior of the creatures inhabiting the islands would confirm the title. Having gone for so long without human contact, the birds and reptiles that inhabit the island retain to this day a basic unconcern, a lack of wariness towards people. Despite the bloody record of the last four centuries, the creatures of the islands still pay little attention to two-legged intruders, treating them as mere obstacles to be circumvented, as ambulatory bits of scenery. Nowhere else in the world does such an attitude prevail so largely among animals. And almost nowhere else are there such creatures! The tortoise of the Galapagos could pass for the ancestors of all tortoises, as a fitting offspring of that Turtle reputed by some societies to be carrying the earth on its back (see Chapter 6, "On Turtle Island"). They are massive creatures, imperturbable, slow of movement, usually silent.

There is no certainty of their maximum size. The largest verified specimens had a shell length of up to 51 inches, and an estimated weight of 550 pounds. One of the most distinctive features of the tortoises, besides their bulk, is their shells. The shells of subspecies vary from island to island. The shape of the shell seems to have been determined by the kinds of food the tortoises eat. The subspecies on Duncan Island have long necks and shells with a high, wide front; and they feed on vegetation above the ground. The tortoises on Indefatigible Island subsist on vegetation found closer to the ground, and the shape of their shells reflects this. There are thought to be about fifteen subspecies of the Galapagos tortoise, each with its own modifications of the basic plan.

Herman Melville vividly captured the impact that the first sight of the creatures has had on generations of sailors. As a young man, he shipped on a vessel that stopped, briefly, in the islands. Several of the tortoises were hauled on board. He recalled, years later, that the tortoises were "black as widower's weeds, heavy as chests of plate, with vast shells medallioned and orbed like shields, and dented and blistered like shields that have breasted a battle—shaggy too, here and there, with dark green moss, and slimy with the spray of the sea. The great feeling inspired by these creatures," he noted, "was that of age:—dateless, indefinite endurance."

As he lay in his hammock that night, Melville recalled, he could hear the "slow, weary draggings" of the creatures along the deck. "Listening to these draggings and concussions, I thought me of the haunt from which they came; as isle full of metallic ravines and gulches, sunk bottomlessly into the hearts of splintered mountains, and covered for many miles with inextricable thickets. I then pictured these three straightforward monsters, century after century, writhing through the shades, grim as blacksmiths; crawling so slowly and ponderously, that not only did toadstools and all fungus things grow beneath their feet, but a sooty mass sprouted upon their backs." (From "The Encantadas," in *The Piazza Tales*, 1856.)

The powerful impression worked on mariners by the sight of these creatures is indicated by Melville's recitation of a "long cherished" superstition held by sailors about the tortoises: "They earnestly believe that all wrecked sea-officers, more especially commodores and captains, are at death transformed into tortoises; thenceforth dwelling upon these hot aridities, sole solitary Lords of Asphatium." While this may be nothing more than a rather airy fancy on Melville's part, one can believe that some such story was at one time circulated among sailors, not a little baffled by what they had seen in the Enchanted Isles. However, such superstitions did not lessen the slaughter.

It is impossible to say what desperate or curious sailors first killed a tortoise and found its flesh to be quite tasty, a welcome relief from shipboard rations. However it might have started, the practice soon became universal. William Dampier, an English pirate, noted in 1684 that the tortoises "are so extraordinarily large and fat, and so sweet, that no pullet eats [i.e., *tastes*] more pleasantly." Seemingly, every ship that stopped at the islands sent parties ashore to collect tortoises. A second unfortunate discovery was soon made. The tortoises could be brought aboard alive, and would remain alive for as much as several months, providing a long-term supply of fresh meat. It was not uncommon to butcher several tortoises on an island, and haul that meat aboard along with living specimens.

Those who slaughtered the tortoises provide a sort of rough maritime history of the past several hundred years. First there were the royal ships of the Spaniards, who discovered the islands in 1535, and who later developed a route for their treasure fleets that passed close by the islands. The treasure fleets, groaning with the riches ripped from the native kingdoms of South America, attracted swarms of privateers and pirates, and they made the Galapagos a frequent stop-over point. Then there were the warships of a variety of nations, sent out on long cruises. The whaling fleets plying the Pacific also made the islands a common stop-over point, thus doing their best to destroy two unique life forms: whales as well as tortoises. The merchant ships plying the Pacific made stops on the islands. Several countries encouraged colonization of the chain, sending in settlers who little knew how unsuited to cultivation the Galapagos were. Finally, and most recently, there were the explorers, and the scientists, sent out by a variety of nations and institutions. Only the last group felt any restraint in slaughtering the tortoises. But while they did not engage in wholesale annihilation of the tortoises, several scientific expeditions did take numbers of them for collections, further depleting the already badly weakened populations. There were few voices raised against the destruction of the Galapagos tortoises, and those who did voice concern came only recently.

The most famous scientist to visit the islands was Charles Darwin, who first observed the giant tortoises in September of 1835. "As I was walking along," he wrote, "I met two large tortoises, each of which must have weighed at least two hundred pounds: one was eating a piece of cactus, and as I approached it stared at me and slowly stalked away; the other gave a deep hiss and drew in his head." (*Voyage of the Beagle*, 1840.)

Thereafter Darwin spent many hours observing the behavior of the tortoises; their travels, feeding, mating, and nesting were included in his observations. This was all fresh, important information: important both in itself, and in its influence on Darwin's thoughts. The Galapagos Islands played an essential role in helping Darwin to develop the theory of evolution. In moments when Darwin was not seriously observing them, he amused himself in a manner long used by visitors to the islands: "I frequently got on their shells, and then giving a few raps on the hinder parts of their shells, they would rise up and walk away. . . ." Of the common use of the tortoises for food, he noted that "the flesh of this animal is largely employed, both fresh and salted; and a beautifully clear oil is prepared from the fat. When a tortoise is caught, the man makes a slit in its tail, so as to see inside its body, whether the fat under the dorsal plate is thick. If it is not, the animal is liberated and it is said to recover from this strange operation."

One cannot say how many tortoises were taken from the islands over these hundreds of years. There are several estimates that place the number in the millions; one estimate suggests some *ten million* tortoises have been killed by men over the past four hundred years. The tortoises have also been adversely affected by the creatures introduced by men: pigs, goats, and rats. All three now exist on many of the islands in large numbers, and all three take tortoise eggs whenever they find them. In addition, they compete with the tortoises for food, for the tortoises are vegetarians, eating grasses, parts of cacti, leaves, berries, lichen, and the fruit of the manchineel tree.

Considering the adversities which the great tortoises have faced, it is remarkable that there are any specimens left at all. Several islands have been depopulated, and the distinct subspecies of those islands are extinct. However, efforts at conservation over the past three decades may have arrested the decline of species on several islands. There is even the possibility that some subspecies have begun to increase in number, to make a spirited comeback. Even their chances, however, are tenuous; expert, constant help will be required for many years to come. We no longer need their flesh, their eggs, or the oil to be gotten from their fat. Considering the havoc we have wreaked on them, it is not asking much that we make amends to do what we can to preserve the remnants of a remarkable, pacific, and perfectly adapted creature.

Caring for Turtles as Pets

I don't keep turtles as pets. I have briefly kept several turtles to more closely observe them and learn about them. After I had learned what I could I released them in the same locations from which I had taken them. Some species of turtles do, of course, make good, tractable, interesting "pets," but they aren't easy to keep, if you want to do it properly. Other turtles don't make good pets at all; and yet other species, increasingly endangered in their native habitats, can only be further damaged by being collected as pets.

I don't keep turtles, and I do not generally feel they should be kept. You can learn a good deal more studying turtles in their original environments. Yet I realize that, no matter what I might say, many people are going to remain intent on having turtles. This chapter is intended to present all of the specific information *necessary* to keep turtles successfully in captivity. The procedures are elaborate enough to discourage all but the most determined of turtle lovers. If you are anxious to keep turtles, but unwilling or unable to follow the procedures, I urge you to reconsider before the matter ends in disappointment for you and death for the turtles.

The continued destruction of natural areas for energy, roads, or homes has caused many once common species to become increasingly rare. Those listed as being endangered in certain states cannot be collected or sold. If you capture a specimen of a rare species, your success can only increase the already intolerable strain upon that species. Before you go searching for turtles, check with your state fish and wildlife department to find out what species are on the endangered list. If you discover any such specimens, watch them, learn what you can about them, and leave them alone. Only if they are in adverse surroundings, such as a suburban street or the middle of a road, should you move them—and then only to take them to a more congenial, natural environment. Should you find a shop selling species listed as endangered, report it. If the owner bought them in ignorance, he will suffer no penalties; and if he bought them in defiance of the law, he deserves to be penalized. A species is destroyed through many small, selfish acts, not through one great inevitable calamity.

As a group, turtles adapt remarkably well to captivity, if they are given appropriate surroundings. However, not all species are well suited for confinement. Some never accept their captivity; they eat sporadically, and soon fall ill and die. Other species are too dangerous, or too demanding, to make very good captives. And with some others, supplying the necessary environment is prohibitively expensive.

Gopher tortoises just don't do well in captivity. The care and the cost of keeping a gopher tortoise for any length of time has kept the animal outside all boundaries but those of zoological centers. The gopher seems to have a real desire for freedom. In captivity it becomes lethargic and susceptible to a variety of infections, including pneumonia, that do not afflict it in the wild. The destruction of much of their habitat, and their once great popularity among wholesale pet suppliers, have pushed this species to the edge of extinction. The remnants are having a hard go of it, and any further pressure exerted by collectors can only push them closer to disappearance.

Snapping turtles also don't make good captives. I say this knowing that there are those who will say, "But what about my friend, and that friendly snapper he had—the one everybody could touch?" There may be some snappers who are models of friendliness and gentility. I have never seen one. Snappers can grow quite large, and the jaws of even small specimens can exert great pressure. Their name was not given in jest. Snappers begin biting as soon as they fight their way out of their eggs, and their aggressive tendencies do not mellow with age—especially when they are outside their native element. They are fast, dangerous animals. If you have children or if, as I do, you have a great fondness for your fingers, steer clear of snappers. Should their very aura of danger attract you, it would be worth keeping in mind that snappers have large appetites—they make a very expensive pet. And they're messy eaters, meaning that their cases will have to be cleaned frequently.

Soft-shelled turtles also have a reputation for sharp temper. I have heard tell of individual softshells that were very amicable creatures; but, as a rule, the various species of softshells can be expected to be abrasive and tough. Softshells are also very fast in water and endowed with sharp claws.

It may still be possible in some areas either to find or buy small specimens of sea turtles. Don't do it. Every species of marine turtle is in trouble today as a result of the ever increasing demand for their eggs, shells, and flesh. None of them do well in captivity. Some may throw themselves against the confines of their cage until they die or burst free. They require rather elaborate machinery to generate a continuous supply of salt water. And we don't know, with certainty, what the species eat. In captivity, they frequently *don't* eat, fasting until they die. You won't learn much about a sea turtle by keeping it captive, except perhaps a chastening lesson in the powerful attraction some creatures have for a free life.

There are still species of North American turtles that are hardy enough, taciturn enough, and plentiful enough to be available as pets. By restricting your collection to such species, you will be taking a hand in helping preserve the rare varieties. And you will not be deprived: many of the species of turtles best fitting the requirements of a pet are just as fascinating, just as capable of surprising, as the rare varieties. Some of them are also just as troublesome.

Shopping for Turtles

For many years great tanks full of baby turtles were a common sight in pet stores. Just as common were the small plastic bowls with a raised area and a brown stalk intended as a palm tree, touted as an excellent home for the babies. It wasn't. The dry "turtle food" carried in most stores was advertised as being a complete diet for a turtle, with perhaps an occasional piece of lettuce tossed in for variety. It wasn't. The history of the production and sale of baby turtles through the pet industry can largely be described in two words: ignorance and greed. Merchandisers of turtles were either unaware, or unwilling to admit, that the turtles they sold had little chance of surviving to adulthood, and that the containers and food they sold were inadequate. Although I know of individual cases in which infant turtles were successfully raised and had long and healthy lives, such remain the exception rather than the rule. Most of the baby turtles hustled in this manner generally survived less than a year.

It is no longer possible to buy a baby turtle. The Food and Drug Administration has banned the sale of any turtle having a shell length of less than four inches, effectively restricting the market to adult turtles. While this is a reprieve for the turtles, it was not done with them primarily in mind. In 1972, the last year in which baby turtles were sold, some fifteen million were produced and purchased, the majority by pet stores. And some 280,000 cases of salmonellosis, a bacterial infection of the intestinal tract, were thought to have been transmitted to humans by some of the newly-bought pet turtles. Salmonella bacteria occur with varying frequency among different species. During the boom days in the pet turtle market, dealers would collect great numbers of turtles and keep them in large tanks, mixing species indiscriminately. Even a few infected specimens could quickly pass on the bacteria to a large group.

By banning the sale of turtles under four inches, the FDA drastically pushed down the number of turtles available to the pet trade. Because of the time and costs required to raise turtles to maturity, most large-scale dealers simply switched to other animals capable of a faster turn-over. Those specimens of chelonians now for sale are frequently collected in the wild, and are adults. Both characteristics make it unlikely that they will be carrying any transferable bacteria. Result: a great drop in the number of cases of salmonellosis thought to be transmitted by turtles. Also, as a result, several species of turtles being pushed toward extinction by the activities of large-scale collectors are now making a modest comeback in their native environments. More importantly, although there are far fewer turtles being bought as pets, those being purchased are much more likely to lead a pleasant, healthy life. Buyers of turtles today generally belong to one of two groups: those who truly want a turtle, or those who've simply made a mistake.

Today there are fewer outlets offering turtles than in 1972. The higher costs involved in obtaining and raising turtles until they are large enough to sell, and the increasing restrictions in species that can be collected have contributed to making the chelonian an infrequent item in pet stores. In many areas you will have to look diligently to find any turtles for sale. If you're fortunate, you may be able to find a pet store in which the operator or owner is a turtle fancier. Such a store, likely to have the widest and healthiest selection of turtles, will prove to be an excellent source of information on turtle care and handling. I have had the good fortune to discover such a store, and the knowledgeable staff there have passed on to me several points on turtle care of which I had not been aware. Stores like this, however, remain few and far between. Unless you know someone who can refer you to such an outlet, you're going to have to do some looking about.

I have visited pet stores to get an impression of the popularity and availability of turtles as pets. Few stores carried them, although the owners of several claimed to be able to supply turtles upon request. Those shops that did occasionally carry turtles restricted their stock to the commonest species, such as box turtles. Only the stores having personnel strongly interested in turtles carried a variety of species. The strongest impression on my tour, however, was of the great variation in care, knowledge, and cleanliness among stores. I discovered stores that were appallingly filthy, and stores that were kept scrupulously clean. I found stores in which the animals were kept in terribly cramped conditions, their cages jammed so tightly together that the creatures were in a constant state of noisy agitation. And I saw stores in which the stock were kept in large, airy quarters.

You can tell a good deal about a pet store just by looking inside. If it seems dirty, disordered, and neglected, its stock of animals is liable to suffer from the same problems. You will, hopefully, have a choice of stores carrying turtles, so that you can select the better managed shops. Because a shop is usually only the next-to-last in a series of stages for an animal, it is possible that a sick animal can be bought, and sold, by an unsuspecting pet dealer. No matter how positive your impressions of a shop, take a close, careful look at the turtles on display. Their eyes should be clear. They should be active, and seem alert. If they are lifted the head and legs of terrestrial species should be retracted. Aquatic species should appear to "swim" vigorously when held. The shell of a turtle should be hard to the touch. If a shell has soft parts, if the eyes are cloudy and its movements listless, if the turtle fails to react when picked up, don't buy it. And don't buy any other turtles in its container: when they are kept together, an infection can spread rapidly from turtle to turtle.

Before you go shopping for a turtle, try to learn as much as you can about chelonians. Study photographs of the species so that you'll have some notion of what a healthy member of a species should look like. And check out as many pet stores as you can before settling on a purchase. Before you buy, ask about a guarantee: the reaction you receive may tell you a good deal about the firm. The degree of responsibility a pet dealer has for the health of his stock has in the past been a hotly debated topic. Now, many stores will accept responsibility for an animal that either sickens or dies within a month of its purchase. However, such a policy cannot be taken for granted. Ask about it.

There are all sorts of pet stores, all varieties of operators. Many have brought an admirable dedication to their work and served to encourage the first, hesitant steps of young people toward a life-long interest in animals. Pet stores in urban areas provide city youngsters with a chance to see, hold, and react to a variety of animals. If you find a dealer who seems honest and knowledgeable, encourage him, and spread the word around. It is in all our interests to encourage the improvement, from within, of a field that has in the past frequently suffered from a dubious image.

On Keeping Turtles: Environment and Food

First of all, it's not easy. To keep turtles healthy and reasonably well adjusted in captivity, you're going to have to spend both time and money working out a proper environment for them—or they will die.

If you give a turtle just the food and water it needs, while neglecting to build it a sufficiently large or interesting container, it may well cease eating, grow weak, and die. Turtles accept death by starvation as an alternative to a dull captivity, as do many wild creatures. They will not endure what is unacceptable. If escape is impossible, they will simply shrug off their life as one who rids himself of an encumbrance.

What a turtle needs are those conditions closest to its natural habitat. Aquatic turtles need water to float, dive, and swim in. This water must be kept reasonably clean and fresh. Such turtles also need a hump of land, or rocks, or a log, to haul out and bask upon. Terrestrial turtles appreciate a terrain of clean soil or sand, and a cave to take refuge in. Both kinds of turtles need sunlight and fresh air. Such basic conditions are mandatory: you should not pick and choose according to your personal preference. The more closely you can duplicate the natural habitat of a species, the more likely will be your success in raising healthy turtles.

You'll need the right sort of container, to begin with. Then you'll need such accessories as a water pump and filter, a heating coil or cable, and some sort of light unit. While few items are marketed specifically for turtles, the types of components you'll need are available in great variety for tropical fish, and will perform as well for turtles. You can make a basic container from scratch and alter it as your needs dictate.

Ideally, you should keep a turtle in a converted aquarium of a size appropriate to the needs of your pet. Forget about bowls or other makeshift containers. Forget about those wretched plastic dishes with the plastic palm trees (always with three fronds) that were once sold everywhere as the ideal homes for baby turtles. Even if you have only a single turtle, and that only four or five inches long, you'll still need a fairly large container. Turtles are used to moving about; a close confinement, in which they can barely turn, is as frustrating to them as it would be to a human.

An aquarium at least 2 feet in length, and 1 foot in depth, would make an excellent container for a single terrestrial turtle. If you have an aquatic species, the aquarium should be at least 1 additional foot in length. If you have, or intend to acquire, several turtles, you'll need a much roomier container. You'll probably have to make it, or have it made for you. If you have the land, you might want to seriously consider keeping your collection of turtles outside. Such a move would require a larger initial investment, but in the long run it is simpler, somewhat easier to maintain, and generally healthier for the turtles. Details on specific environments for indoor and outdoor maintenance are given in the following sections.

Turtles don't eat just one kind of food in their native habitats. They can't afford to, for most species are rarely in locations where a single food source is both very abundant and perpetual. As one food source is exhausted, or disappears with the changing seasons, they must turn to others, drawing nutrition from whatever is available, taking advantage of whatever turns up.

It is important that you reproduce such a diet for captive turtles. It is highly unlikely that just one food, no matter how nutritious, will supply all the vitamins and minerals that the turtles require. Being fed on the same bland diet, day in, day out, may also demoralize the turtles, even cause them to lose interest in eating. Boredom is the major danger one runs by feeding turtles "turtle-pellets," sold in pet shops under a variety of trade names. While such pellets do contain a somewhat balanced diet, they make for particularly uninteresting meals. Turtles may seem to have overwhelming patience, but in fact they (like all other creatures) are capable of being bored and dissatisfied, and of descending from such a state into melancholy and illness. In addition, the pellets do not provide sufficient fiber (roughage), and turtles are prone to serious constipation under such conditions.

What you feed them depends on two points: what each species prefers, and the degree of energy you can muster. Different kinds of turtles eat different foods. You can find out what their specific preferences by checking in the reference works listed in the Bibliography. I am aware of some keepers-of-turtles who collect the food for their captives from the wilds, taking earthworms, beetles, crickets, snails, grasshoppers, grubs, bloodworms, tubifex worms, and small fish from field and stream. This certainly gives the turtles a very fresh and varied diet, but it can also be exhausting and difficult to collect. Bloodworms and tubifex worms may be available from a supply house or well-stocked pet store in your area. As for the rest, I think the best practice is to substitute similar items for the wild diet. Aquatic turtles, being more carnivorous than some terrestrial turtles, appreciate a greater percentage of meat, like chopped beef, beef heart or kidneys, and chopped raw fish. Ernst and Barbour have indicated success in raising aquatic turtles on a prepared diet of "canned fish (usually salmon and mackerel), liquid multiple vitamins, and powdered bone meal. The vitamins are added—mixing thoroughly—at the rate of 15 cc per 2 pound of fish and the bone meal at the rate of 3 tablespoons per 2 pound of fish" (p. 280). Lettuce, carrots, other vegetables, and fruits (e.g., bananas) should also be included in the diet.

Terrestrial turtles, such as box or wood turtles, should be fed beef, lettuce, "tomatoes, apples, bananas, watermelon, canteloupe . . . and hard boiled eggs. Vitamins and bone meal should be added to this diet" (p. 281). Cooked sweet potatoes, raw squash, peaches, and corn can also be given.

Tortoises don't need, or like, much meat in their diet. Instead, they prefer a variety of vegetables and fruits, including "lettuce, cabbage, spinach, tomatoes, bananas, grapes, watermelon, cantaloupe, and apples" (p. 281). In addition, Ernst and Barbour note that tortoises will also take bread, hard boiled eggs, and eggshells, and that they have a special fondness for yellow flowers (such as dandelions). Vitamins and minerals should also be mixed into their food.

Giving turtles regular doses of vitamins and minerals is essential. Specifically, turtles need vitamins A, B, C, and D, and a large regular supply of calcium and phosphorus. Some of these nutrients, of course, will be found in the foodstuffs, but not a steady amount that you can depend on. Several preparations of calcium and phosphorus, and a variety of liquid vitamins, should be available at pet shops dealing in reptiles. Powdered oyster shell, available from food stores, can be mixed into the food of large adult tortoises and aquatic turtles.

The idea is to provide a variety of foods. Watch the turtles to determine if they have certain favorites or if there are foods that they consistently ignore. Don't let them become dependent on any foods that are available only in season: it is sometimes hard to get a turtle to accept different foods in place of its accustomed diet.

Feed adult turtles daily. If they are not very active, feed them only every other day. (If they are not very active, they probably need a larger container.) Hatchlings and young turtles should be fed every day. The food should be given to them no earlier than mid-morning, no later than early afternoon. Because turtles like to stretch out their meals (indeed, in the wild they spend many hours searching out food), their food should be left in their containers for several hours. Never let food remain overnight. Remove any food that has been standing in direct sunlight for any length of time; meat can spoil and fruits turn sour in warm, bright conditions. Place the food in some sort of bowl for terrestrial turtles or tortoises. When feeding aquatic turtles, turn off the filtering system in the tank so that food particles do not stop it up.

Prepare the food for your pet turtles as if it were for your own table. Thoroughly wash all of the vegetables you give them; wash and peel the fruits; and clean any fish. Don't use anything that you suspect of being spoiled. Chop all the food given turtles into small, bite-size pieces. While some texts recommend using dog food instead of beef cubes, I hesitate to do so. Some dog foods are fatty, others are greasy or contain ash. It's certainly cheaper to use dog food, especially if you've got aquatic turtles, but I'm not sure that it's better.

The ability of turtles to anticipate their feeding time has been frequently remarked upon. Terrestrial turtles or tortoises have been known to congregate in the spot in which they are usually fed at that time of the day when they are usually fed. Aquatic turtles have also been observed to become distinctly excited, even agitated, as their feeding time approached. If for no other reason than not to disappoint the turtles, try to feed them at about the same time every day.

Keeping Terrestrial Turtles Outdoors

Keeping turtles in an outdoor enclosure allows them a spacious confinement, plenty of sunlight, and environmental conditions close to those of their native habitats. It is thus probably the best method for keeping turtles in captivity. It is not, however, the easiest or the least expensive; just the best.

Of course, you may not be able to build an outdoor enclosure, even if you wish to do so. To keep turtles in a comfortable confinement outdoors you need a good plot of land and some prospects of permanence. Dwellers in cities have, generally, neither. It is no use committing yourself to such a project unless you're determined to make it a long-standing avocation— unless you're ready to devote time each day, year in, year out, to properly maintain the turtles.

An outdoor enclosure is a plot of land fenced in so as to discourage the turtle's escape attempts. Within the enclosure should be a cave or some other artificial construction to provide shelter for the turtles. It is somewhat less expensive to build an enclosure for terrestrial than for aquatic turtles, since terrestrial turtles do not require a large pool. You can build an outdoor enclosure during a long day, or over a weekend, and you have a great deal of leeway in designing it. There are three essential features: adequate space, shelter, and a small shallow pool. You can use whatever design is most pleasing to you, provided that these conditions are met. Consider the "terrarium" as another part of your garden, work it into the prevailing shape and appearance of your land, or create something different enough to provide a pleasing contrast.

As most turtles are not determined climbers, you need not make the fencing of their enclosure especially high. Of course, if you have a fenced-in garden or yard, you need do nothing else. Give the turtles the run of the place. An expanse to explore will surely please their sense of curiosity. If you have no fence, or if you prefer to restrict the movements of the turtles somewhat, you will have to erect a low wire wall. The wire fencing that is sold in garden supply centers and intended to fence off flower beds is quite adequate for confining the turtles. The mesh of such fencing is somewhat open—not wide enough for an adult turtle or tortoise to squeeze through, but wide enough to attract their attention and keep most species more interested in poking their heads through than in trying to burrow under. Some species of turtles are diggers of burrows. Other individual turtles, though burrowing is not common in their species, dig burrows out of some private motivation. You can circumvent the problem of turtles' digging their way out by extending the wire fencing to several inches below the surface. Excavate a narrow trench, at least 3 inches deep, all along the perimeter of the intended enclosure. Drop the fencing in place, standing it along the bottom of the trench. The fencing material should be 6 inches in height, so that at least three inches of it will be above ground. Drive in thin wooden stakes at regular intervals along the trench and nail the fencing to them. Shovel the soil you've removed back into place. While the wire holds the fence firmly in place, it is spaced at sufficiently short intervals so that the part penetrating beneath the soil will form points too narrow for the turtles to dig through.

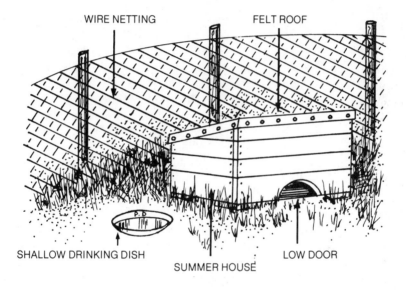

WIRE NETTING   FELT ROOF

SHALLOW DRINKING DISH   LOW DOOR

SUMMER HOUSE

Outdoor Enclosure for Terrestrial Species

The best manner in which to provide water for the turtles or tortoises is to dig a hole within the enclosure and sink in a basin or a plastic pan. This container will have to be big enough to provide sufficient water for all the turtles, and sufficient space for all of them to enter and bask in the water. Thus it need not be deep, but it should be wide. The container you use should not be susceptible to rust. Bring the soil around it right up to the rim, so that the turtles will not have to reach up over any barrier for the water. Check it every day to make certain that it remains level with the ground. If you are keeping tortoises, the water in the container should be no more than three inches deep. Any more, and the tortoises could drown. Terrestrial turtles can handle somewhat deeper water. Change the water frequently; don't allow debris to build up in the bottom.

Building a proper shelter takes the most time. The turtles need a place in which they can take refuge when they feel the urge to do so. They also need a shelter to withdraw into during the night, during cold or rainy weather, or when the sun is too intense. You can build a shelter with wood, or shape one with rocks and cement. A cave made of rocks has the advantage of looking more natural, whereas a wooden house can be moved about and is somewhat easier to clean.

Almost any sort of large wooden box will do, so long as it is in good shape and not missing any slats. You can remove an entire side to provide access; or, better yet, cut out a sufficiently wide door. The door should be half again as wide as the widest member of your collection. Short, stout legs should be fitted to the box, so that it can stand off the ground. Doing so will keep the floor from becoming damp. Use a light-color, lead-free paint to paint the interior; give the exterior two coats of an oil paint. The roof will have to be weatherproofed. A suitably large piece of thick plastic or polyvinyl should be firmly attached to the exterior of the roof and cut to overlap the side walls by an inch. This will prevent rain from running off of the roof and into any cracks at the points where the walls join the roof. Whether you use nails or staples to hold the plastic in place, check afterwards to make certain that no sharp points are projecting into the box. A turtle can receive a severe scratch, even a deep wound, from a nail head. To keep cold drafts or rain out, a piece of clear flexible material, such as Mylar plastic, is necessary to cover the opening. The covering must be light enough to be easily pushed up by a turtle, with sufficient spring to fall back into place after the turtle has entered. By cutting the covering into fairly thin strips, you'll make it easier for the turtles to shoulder the material aside.

Because the unit stands up off of the ground, you'll have to provide a ramp up to the door of the box. The ramp can be made of wood. Small strips of wood should be nailed to it in a pattern resembling a series of ascending V's; the idea is to provide grips for the turtles to haul themselves upwards. Give the ramp as gentle a slope as you can.

The house should be cleaned out regularly. Spreading a thin layer of straw along the bottom will make it easier to clean out any wastes. I know of one collector who provided the roof of such a house with hinges and a hook. The hinges allowed him simply to open the roof to clean the place out, and the hook kept the roof immovable at all other times.

These instructions might seem demanding or over-elaborate; but turtles are not automatons or senseless brutes. You can keep them under much less careful conditions than have been described. But they will suffer if deprived of sufficient sunlight, water, shelter, space, or (also essential) variety in environment. If they are deprived they will be discontented, more prone to becoming ill, and will likely suffer from the chelonian equivalent of melancholy. At times it seems to me that the stolid appearance of the turtle is its greatest weakness, as it lends itself to the belief that such creatures are simple machines devoid of more subtle properties. They are not simply an organic motor laid between two plates of shell. Treat them as if they were, as if they can compensate for any deficiency in their surroundings, and they will likely die, sooner rather than later.

If you're willing to keep turtles, if you really want to keep them, do it properly or, for the benefit of both parties, don't do it at all.

Keeping Fresh-Water Turtles Outdoors

Aquatic turtles require a pool, construction of which is the major expense and a major source of effort. The size of the pool you'll need for keeping aquatic turtles depends on the number of turtles you intend to keep. Its shape is largely a matter of personal taste. The pool must be at least 8 inches in depth; it should be at least 5 feet long and at least 4 feet wide. These are minimum requirements: the larger you can make the pond, the better. There is no such thing as too much space for captive aquatic turtles. The shape need not be elaborate—a simple oval will do.

The bottom and walls of the pond can be of poured concrete, or can be made of a plastic liner fitted over the walls of the excavation. Recently, lightweight molded garden ponds have become available, some of which are sufficiently long and deep; it may be hard, however, to find one of sufficient width. A molded pool, or a liner, is less permanent, easy to dismantle, should that become necessary. A concrete pool is permanent; it would be almost as costly to dismantle as to install. I urge you to think long and hard on your plans, and on the degree of your interest in turtles, before making the decision to dig up your backyard.

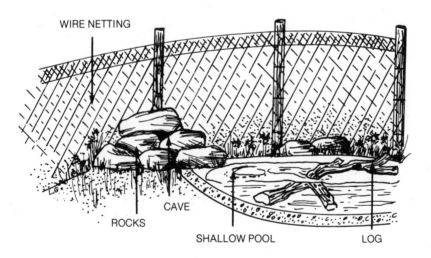

WIRE NETTING

CAVE

ROCKS

SHALLOW POOL

LOG

Outdoor Enclosure for Aquatic Species

Because aquatic turtles both feed and excrete in the water, a good drainage system is vital. Without one, the water would soon become fetid or rife with highly infectious debris.

The pool must be located in a spot receiving direct sunlight through most of the day. However, one portion of it should also include an area with some sort of overlay so that a shaded spot is always available for the turtles. On very bright summer days, the water in the pond may become dangerously hot. The overhang will provide some refuge for the turtles. Adding cooler water at intervals during the day will also help.

Some portion of land should also be included in the design, giving the pool a border of soil all around its edges. If the turtles you're keeping are prone to occasionally emerge from the water, and prowl around, you'll have to provide a sufficiently wide margin to allow for their peregrinations. Don't leave this land barren. Design a rock garden and plant it with grass or dig it out and lay in clean sand. As with an enclosure for terrestrial turtles, the point is to make the pool a part of the landscape in harmony with the design of your yard. While plants would be placed in tubs and placed in the pool, the turtles will likely trim the leaves, and their movements will upset all but the most sturdily anchored of pots.

For basking, a pile of logs, or rocks, should be built up in the center of the pond. The basking area is essential. It should be large enough to accommodate all of the turtles. By placing it in the center of the pool, you'll encourage even the shyest of the turtles to feel secure enough to come out and bask.

There is one particular problem associated with keeping turtles outdoors, and no very clear solution to it. Raccoons, cats, dogs, and children will all likely be drawn to the enclosure. Though a strong, high fence will help, vigilance will still be necessary. Children provide the least manageable problem. They should be cautioned about the rather sensitive nature of turtles. If they understand that their carrying away of a turtle might cause its death, they may be less likely to attempt it. However, reason alone may not be adequate. You're going to have to remain on guard. There is a further danger here: although a pool in which aquatic turtles are kept is only a few inches deep, it is deep enough for a small child to drown in. The measures you take to protect the turtles, and the children, will necessarily depend on your local situation. The point is that some measures will have to be taken—and maintained.

Keeping Fresh-Water Turtles Indoors

If you can do so, I recommend that you keep aquatic turtles outdoors. To create an enclosure for them, as previously described, is admittedly neither inexpensive nor effortless. It does, however, greatly simplify their care. To keep an aquatic turtle indoors, you'll need a large container, sturdy enough to hold quite a few gallons of water. You'll have to filter the water, and you'll have to heat it.

Large aquariums are often the first container turtle fanciers think of. If they allow a turtle enough room, they are acceptable. However, their shape does not allow for much experimentation in layout; there aren't many places in which you can put an area for the turtles to haul out upon. Most aquariums are long, but the best design for aquatic turtles is a container that is long *and* shallow: turtles don't need a deep container so much as they need a roomy one in which they can move around without being cramped.

Shop around for an appropriate container. Aquariums are now produced in such a wide range of sizes that you may be able to find just the shape and size you need. If you cannot, you can settle for the aquarium that comes closest to suiting your needs. Or you can have a custom-made unit built. Or, you can use your ingenuity to design your own, or to adapt some existing container to the task. You might, for instance, be able to turn a child's wading pool into an excellent habitat for aquatic turtles. The primary difficulty in using a shallow pool is rigging up some sort of enclosure along its margins to prevent any turtles from clambering out.

No matter what sort of container you select, you're going to have to keep the water in it warm and fresh. To do this, you'll need a heater and filtering equipment. you can find both in stores carrying aquarium equipment and supplies. To secure the right heater, you'll have to know the amount of water your container holds. Heaters are designed to maintain warmth for specific amounts of water. If you're using an aquarium, the heater will clamp easily in place. However, if you're using some other sort of container, having thicker walls than the relatively thin-walled aquarium, you'll have to rig some sort of supplementary attachment to hold the heater in place. It is vitally important that the water be maintained at a steady temperature. Turtles kept in unheated or inadequately heated water, especially during the winter months, will surely catch cold, and surely die.

The water must also be kept clean. To do this, it must be filtered. You'll need a pump and a filter to properly do the job. There are a variety of aquarium pumps; you should be able to find one suited to the volume of water in your container. Other pumps, such as those designed for fountains, may also be adapted to the tank. The set-up you must establish will pull water out of the habitat, pass it through a filter, and pour it, cleaned of impurities, back into the container.

Waste materials build up rapidly in water. Scattered bits of food and eliminated wastes can quickly form a foul-smelling scum, coating the basking areas, the turtles, and the entire surface of the water. Such debris is particularly rich in bacteria that can infect, sicken, and even kill the turtles. You can avoid part of the problem by removing turtles from the container for feeding. The difficulty with such a procedure is that such daily handling may greatly disturb some of the shyer species of aquatic turtles. Further, many turtles are gradual feeders, preferring to take some food, go away, come back to feed, and go away again: such a process can take several hours. Forced into a rigid schedule, turtles may be unable to take in sufficient food, or they may even develop digestive problems. For such reasons it would be preferable to install a better filtering system, thus avoiding the necessity of removing the turtles.

After you've installed the heating and filtering units, run them for several days before putting the turtles in the container. If the systems aren't functioning properly, you'll have a chance to catch the problem, and correct it, before any harm can be done.

Within the pool, or aquarium, you'll need an area of rock, small logs, or other material large enough for all of the turtles to climb onto for basking. This material should be devoid of any surfaces rough enough to scratch a turtle's plastron or limbs. If the surface of the rock or log is very steep, you'll have to provide steps up to it. A series of flat rocks, laid one upon the other in order of descending size (the smallest rock being at the top), will allow the turtles easy ascent and a variety of spots on which to bask. If you're keeping more than one aquatic turtle, be certain that the basking area is large enough to accommodate all at the same time. Many species seem to prefer communal basking; they will squeeze together in one location when other equally good but empty locations are available nearby. If you're using more than one piece to make the basking area, use a strong cement to bind the pieces together.

Cover the bottom of the container with a layer of aquarium pebbles deep enough so that it cannot be seen. While plants add considerably both to the appearance and diversity of the habitat, it may be difficult to keep them for any length of time. Turtles are habitual nibblers and culinary explorers—they'll sample anything in the tank that looks vaguely edible, and they'll probably give plants an especially thorough working over. Floating aquatic plants, such as water hyacinths, may be left undisturbed. They add a pleasing effect to a container, and they also provide shelter for the turtles. (Hiding is a normal part of aquatic turtles' behavior. While they need no longer do it to secure food, they seem to enjoy doing so.) Adding plants to the habitat or some other area (such as an artificial cave) in which the turtles can hide will be both decorative and practical. The same basic rule applies to aquatic habitats as to all other habitats created for turtles: make it interesting by giving it variety. Dull, sterile, simple habitats are uninteresting to observe, and deadly boring for the turtles. If nothing else will work, you can add plastic plants to the unit, anchoring them in the gravel on the bottom.

The turtles, and any real plants you might add, need sunlight or a bright substitute for it. They need a lot of it. For a large unit, you'll need a 150-watt light mounted on a flexible stand. Position the light so that it is about 2½ feet above the basking site. While it need not be directly over the basking area, it should be placed at a very steep angle to it. Keeping this in mind, you might want to build the basking site rather close to the wall of the unit (but not so close that the turtles could use the site as a stepping-stone to escape). Of course, the light will need to be well anchored so that there is no chance of it tipping into the water. In a location receiving no direct sunlight, the light will have to be run for eight hours a day.

Running a light, a heating unit, and a pump and filter system is going to have a noticeable effect on your utility bill. It is not possible to calculate beforehand the precise additional cost you will face; but once you have the turtles, you cannot economize in the matter of energy. If you do not run the appliances every day, you can't succeed in keeping aquatic turtles indoors.

Keeping Terrestrial Turtles Indoors

You have a good deal more latitude in designing an indoor habitat for terrestrial species than you do for aquatic species. Some families having a single box turtle as a pet allow it the run of the house and report no difficulties with the arrangement. The variety of nooks and crannies in a house into which a turtle can withdraw are very pleasing to it. However, you'll have to make certain that there are no sharp or dangerous surfaces capable of harming an inquisitive tortoise. And you'll still have to provide fresh water and a warm spot to bed down in at night. This doesn't mean simply a box with an old blanket. During the winter months, if the turtle is not hibernating, it will need heated quarters at night, and perhaps even throughout very cold days. Even in a well-heated home, the floors and those areas just above them are often much colder than the prevailing room temperatures. Even a brief exposure to the cold could cause a turtle to come down with pneumonia. Probably the best solution to this danger is to keep the tortoise in a vivarium throughout the cold months, giving it the run of the house only in warm weather.

A vivarium is any artificial habitat in which amphibians or reptiles are kept. Some stores carry vivariums, made of tin sheets fastened to a metal frame or of glass held in place by a wooden frame. You can quite easily make your own vivarium, using sheets of plastic, or panes of glass, along with wood. Or you can convert a sufficiently large aquarium to a vivarium, replacing water with pebbles and plants.

Warmth is as important to land turtles as to aquatic species, so some sort of heat source will be needed. A bright light, suspended over the unit, may be sufficient to double as a heat source, especially if the vivarium is located close to a radiator. You're going to have to supply the turtle(s) with the optimal temperatures to which they are accustomed—generally temperatures in the low or mid 70s (°F). And, unless the specimens hibernate, you're going to have to maintain this steady temperature throughout the year. Using a vivarium with transparent walls of glass or plastic and giving it a location receiving direct sunlight will certainly help, although it will not be altogether adequate. You could bury a heating cable in the gravel covering the bottom of a vivarium. Or you could create a special enclosure within the unit, a square "room" having walls of Mylar plastic strips, loose enough to give way before the turtles, but sufficiently resilient to fall back into place. Keep the water dish within this room, and direct a light into it. The Mylar, the light, and the water will combine to make the room both warm and moist, providing an excellent retreat for the turtles.

Cover the floor of the vivarium with a thick layer of clean, smooth pebbles. While earth would give a vivarium a much more natural look, the pebbles are easier to remove and clean. And clean it you must. Every few days, you'll have to replace the gravel to prevent bacteria and noisome odors from making the unit unlivable. You can cut down on the cost of purchasing gravel by washing what you remove, rinsing it with boiling water, allowing it to dry, and returning it to the unit. In this way you can make do with your initial purchase of gravel. You can reduce the job somewhat by using a piece of tile or a rubber mat cut to size for feeding. Sink it into the gravel, to floor level, and place the food upon it. After the turtles have taken as much of the food as they seem to want, remove the mat, clean it, and hold it aside until the next feeding.

Even confirmed land turtles, who rarely enter flowing water, like to bask in water. You can either provide a large dish of water for the unit or, if there is not sufficient space, remove the turtles and place them in a separate container of lukewarm water for several baths each week. Once a week you can add a dose of a sulfa lotion to the water, making the bath both relaxing and hygienic. Change the water in the water dish daily. Sink the dish into the pebbles so that its lip is at floor level, making it easy for the turtles to drink. Turtles and tortoises do not discriminate between drinking water and bathing water, so it's not unusual to find a turtle sitting contentedly in the water dish. When this happens, change the water before any other turtles can drink from it.

All species of turtles appreciate having a refuge nearby. There are times when they seem to need the reassuring sensation of being sheltered, so it is important not to frustrate their desire. Secretiveness, the drive to camouflage one's presence, is an important component of many species' behavior. Give them some sort of artificial cave into which they can withdraw. If you're keeping more than one terrestrial turtle, make the shelter large enough to accommodate all of them at once so that no contest for possession need ensue.

As with habitats for aquatic species, there is no reason to have a dull, sterile vivarium. As room allows, sink some potted plants into the pebbles. If the walls of the unit are sufficiently high, build a pile of rocks broad enough to allow the turtles to climb and bask. Use your imagination to create as varied and interesting a habitat as you can. It is essential that the habitat provide warmth and sunlight. How it is provided, and in what setting, is up to you.

Diseases and Cures

"Aren't turtles dirty?" I've heard that question asked over and over again by people who've never had turtles, but who suspect the worst. I don't know precisely how the idea originated, how turtles became identified with uncleanliness and, by implication, transmittable diseases, but it seems to have achieved a certain currency. Turtles, however, aren't "dirty"—at least no more so than any other wild creatures. And they are rarely culpable in the transmission of diseases to people: *more often, we make them sick.* I suspect that much of the confusion, at least recently, has its origin in the issue of salmonellosis, a gastrointestinal infection caused by bacteria. While it is rarely fatal (about 3% of those affected die), it does cause real misery, including abdominal pain and periods of intense vomiting or diarrhea. Because the problem has rarely been clearly explained, the impression has been created that, in some mysterious manner, baby turtles are the most common carrier of the bacteria. It is not so.

There are at least 650 strains of salmonella bacterium; chickens, hogs, turkeys, horses, cattle, rodents, and, yes, even cats and dogs may transmit some strains of the bacteria. (The chicken you're preparing for dinner may yet be harboring the bacteria. However, salmonella are destroyed by heat; thoroughly cooking the fowl will make it entirely safe. Many cases of "food poisoning"—an elusive, all-embracing term—are in fact caused by salmonella, surviving the inadequate preparation of the food.) During the boom years in baby turtle sales, it is certainly true that cases of salmonella poisoning, especially among children, did greatly increase, and that these turtles were the source of the problem. But why? The reason is especially revealing of at least one facet of the since-diminished wholesale pet trade. Some large wholesale suppliers of turtles got into the practice of feeding their merchandise offal and meat scraps collected from slaughter houses. This is against the law. It is also a very cheap way of feeding masses of baby turtles. (Expediency sometimes won out over legality.) Such refuse is especially infested with salmonella bacteria. The turtles eat it, and are infected. In addition, it is possible that turtles have their own version of the bacteria, which do not affect them, but which they carry. At least, they usually do not affect the turtles. But if numbers of turtles are kept in water that is not changed, the bacteria build up to such a degree that they are infected. The occurrence of salmonella in turtles, then, reflects largely the way in which captives have been handled.

Since the United States government has banned the sale of infant turtles as pets, the problem has been mostly eliminated; but the memory lingers on, giving turtles a mistaken image, as the Typhoid Marys of the reptile world. Because sales are now restricted to adult turtles, the cost of a turtle has climbed ever higher. Adult turtles are not easy to collect in large numbers. And they cost more to take care of. Conceivably, these facts, though explaining why turtles are scarcer in the trade, assure that those available are healthier. The more you invest in a product, the more careful (hopefully) will be your handling of it. Though it is possible that some turtles now being sold yet harbor the bacteria, this need not be a cause for great alarm. Salmonella, powerful as it is, can be easily avoided. After you've handled a turtle, or cleaned its container, scrub your hands thoroughly with soap and hot water. Do that, and it's unlikely that you'll ever be troubled. If you have children, impress the need for this procedure on them. Only by touching your mouth or handling food after having handled a turtle or changed its water can the bacteria reach you. You can put further distance between your family and the problem by avoiding pet shops which display turtles in particularly crowded and dirty conditions. A turtle coming out of such a situation has a good chance of carrying a heavy dose of salmonella. Such dealers just don't deserve your patronage.

Turtles are vulnerable to a variety of maladies. All are far easier to avoid than to treat. Colds, pneumonia, fungus, diarrhea, constipation, inflamed eyes, and soft shell may all be said to have a common origin: they occur because you've done something wrong. Not because you meant to, not even because you've been especially lax in caring for them. But when you adopt a creature as a pet, you must necessarily assume great responsibility for it. In the wild, a turtle can take shelter when it finds the atmosphere too cold or too hot. It can leave an unsatisfactory environment. In captivity, it depends on you to maintain an acceptable environment. In the wild, it can secure the diet it needs. In captivity, it must be supplied with a balanced diet, rich in the necessary nutrients and sufficient roughage.

Turtles are most likely to catch a cold when they've been either exposed to a prolonged cold draft or kept in a location that is simply too cold for them. Restlessness, an unwillingness to eat, audibly wheezy breathing, even runny eyes or a runny nose, are symptoms of a cold. If left untreated, they can develop into pneumonia and prove fatal.

Examine the conditions under which the turtle has been kept. If necessary, move the turtle to a warmer, sunnier, less drafty location. Generally, turtles from warm environments transported into colder climes are more susceptible to such difficulties. Antibiotics like penicillin, tetracycline, and Aureomycin® (chlortetracycline) are all effective in handling a chelonian cold. Tetracycline is available in pet stores carrying supplies for tropical fish, as it is also useful in treating diseases in fish. Aureomycin and penicillin are available only by prescription from a veterinarian. I admit that one might feel rather foolish taking a turtle to a doctor—but it's the best step if the turtle is ill. Many veterinarians have not had much experience with reptiles, but they can write out a prescription for you and explain how to administer the medicine. When you buy a turtle, it might prove worthwhile to find out which of your local veterinarians has some knowledge of reptiles and their maladies. The symptoms indicating that a turtle has a cold only occur when the infection is already settled in. When that happens, you just don't have time to wait about with the hope that the turtle might spontaneously recover. It won't. It will get worse, if left untreated, and die.

Turtles don't like to be forced to open their mouths. They do it under their own volition, or not at all, suspecting the motives of anyone intent on prying their jaws apart. So how do you give a sick turtle medicine? It isn't easy. First you'll have to dissolve the medicine in water. Penicillin is available as a syrup, and need not be diluted. Whatever medicine you're using, administer the right dose with a sterile eyedropper; use a flat, smooth piece of wood (such as a popsicle stick) to *gently* pry open the turtle's jaws. He will do most of the work for you, reluctantly opening his mouth for the dose. Squeeze out the liquid as far back in the turtle's throat as you can. It may be necessary to hold the turtle's jaws shut for several minutes to prevent it from spitting the medicine out. You may also be able to disguise the medicine, mixing it into the turtle's food. Of course, if the turtle is not eating, or is eating only a little, this will not suffice.

Aquatic turtles are susceptible to fungus infections if their water is allowed to become too cool. Very dirty water also encourages the spread of a fungus. An afflicted turtle will have whitish growths sprouting on its shell or on its limbs, and may have a bright yellow clump around its jaws. Algae, which frequently develop on turtles in the wild, are harmless. Fungi are not. If left untreated, they can kill. Placing infected individuals in a container of salt water (using lukewarm water and table salt, mixing in the salt until the water has a very briny taste) for 15 minutes twice a day will serve as a stopgap measure until you can secure a more powerful remedy. Fish fungicides, available in pet shops, can also be used on turtles. An ointment or bath preparation having sulfa is very effective. Some turtle collectors give their pets a weekly bath in a container of water to which a sulfa mix has been added. Several firms now manufacture liquid sulfa preparations intended specifically for turtles. Whenever you give a turtle any sort of therapeutic bath, make certain that the temperature of the bath water is the same as that maintained in its container—not hotter, and certainly not cooler. If fungus occurs, you've got to clean the container as well as the turtle. Empty it, scrub it out with soap and hot water, rinse it thoroughly, then add a small amount of a fungicide.

Dirty water may also be responsible for inflammations of the eye. The turtle bath mentioned above, composed of warm water and a sulfa preparation (such as sulfathiazole) is of some help in ending the inflammation which is caused by a bacteria. Puffy skin around the eyes, bulging eyes, or eyes that are constantly half-shut are all indications of the problem. Ointments are available in some pet stores. Your veterinarian may be able to prescribe one. A liquid preparation of Chloromycetin® (chloramphenicol) may also be employed. You can use a cotton swab or a sterile eyedropper to apply a liquid—but you must get the medicine right into the eye. An ointment must also be applied directly to the eye. It must be done with caution and gentleness, and without pressure being applied. Rub the ointment onto the eye, but don't lean down or press in; just rub across gently. A cotton swab or your (clean) finger may work. Aquatic turtles being treated for eye inflammation should be kept out of water for several hours after each application (generally, one a day). Use this time to thoroughly scrub out the tank. Get rid of all the water in the tank and add fresh water. Recheck the diet you've been giving the turtle to make sure that it is not lacking in any of the vital nutrients.

It is worthwhile to keep an antibiotic ointment on hand to treat small cuts or abrasions on a turtle's skin or shell. The skin of a reptile is slow to heal, and thus very vulnerable to infection. If the materials you've used in making a container have rough surfaces, if basking rocks or logs you've supplied have a coarse, uneven texture, or if the bottom material in a tank for aquatic turtles is very rough, the turtles can quickly scrape themselves raw. If bacteria or fungi are present in the container, the wound can become much more serious. You can avoid such complications by being very selective in the matter of collecting materials for the container. If anything you're considering using for the interior has a rough surface, look for a less dangerous, smooth substitute. Use an antiseptic to wash any abrasions, then rub on an antibiotic ointment. If none is available, use iodine, or any healing ointment. If the turtle is an aquatic species, keep it out of the water until the ointment has dried and had some chance to penetrate. Clean and treat the wound daily.

Try to identify the cause of the injury, and remove it immediately.

A serious wound calls for more prolonged attention. Use a sterile gauze pad to continuously wipe the wound until bleeding has ceased. Tourniquets don't work on reptiles; they only further damage tissue, and may even affect bones, so don't attempt to use one. After the bleeding has ceased, dilute an antiseptic (such as hydrogen peroxide) in water to make a weak solution. Clean the wound. Use gauze to cover the wound, and sticking plaster, or surgical tape, to hold the dressing in place. Change the dressing frequently enough to prevent its becoming soiled. As soon as the cut is dry, leave the bandage off and cover the surface of the wound with ointment. Again, you must keep aquatic turtles out of the water for several hours after the ointment has been applied, to allow it to dry in place.

I suspect that most of the baby turtles sold in this country survived only a short time after they were purchased. And the major cause of death was undoubtedly soft shell. Soft shell is a deficiency disease, occurring in turtles receiving a diet having insufficient amounts of nutrients, and especially an insufficient amount of calcium. A diet of "turtle pellets" and lettuce is not adequate. Lacking calcium and other nutrients, the bones and shell of a turtle literally go soft. The problem is an especially serious one for young turtles, who are constantly in need of vital nutrients to fuel their growth. The softening generally begins at the rear of the carapace and moves forward. Gently probe your turtle's shell at least once a week for any sign of softening. Once the problem is well advanced, it can only result in death. Yet there is no need for this affliction to occur. If you give a turtle a diet having foods rich in vitamins C and D, *and* a vitamin supplement, and if you give it a particularly sunny location, you're not going to have to worry about soft shell. If it does occur, improve the turtle's diet immediately. Increase the amount and frequency of vitamins. Concentrate on daily doses of calcium: add it to the turtle's water; add it to the food; and, if it's an aquatic turtle, add it to the tank. Don't worry about going to excess; for a turtle with a soft shell, there's no such thing as too much calcium. Bathe it daily in any of the mixtures prepared especially for turtles. Most contain calcium salts as well as an antibiotic. Or just start your turtle off right with a balanced, vitamin and mineral rich diet, and you'll never have to worry about soft shell.

A diet of pellets and lettuce is not only nutritionally a disaster, but also often causes constipation. This is not simply uncomfortable to the turtle—it can become quite serious. If you give your turtle a varied diet, with plenty of roughage, any difficulty can be avoided. If it's too late to avoid the problem, change the diet immediately to include a variety of foods (see section on feeding for recommended items). Get rid of those wretched pellets. And give the turtle a soaking in a shallow container of lukewarm water. Allow him to move about in it until the water begins to cool; then remove him. If the room is chilly or drafty, dry the turtle off and get him back into his container. Such a bath specifically encourages elimination and is generally helpful as a tonic.

Giving a turtle the wrong sorts of food can cause diarrhea. More often, the malady is caused by temperatures that are too low or by a continual draft. It may be a symptom of a cold. Check the turtle's diet to be certain that it isn't receiving foods it shouldn't have. Check the temperature in and around the container. Make certain that the turtle is receiving sufficient doses of vitamins. Keep a close watch for several days for any further signs of illness. You might also try altering the diet for a week or two, substituting foods of equal nutritional value for what you've been giving the turtle. Starchy foods will often help reduce the problem, but are harmful in other ways. Don't use them, except as an emergency measure. And use them sparingly.

Purchased turtles (like those in the wild) may be infested with worms, varieties of small intestinal parasites. Turtles raised in captivity, or captured and shipped out by a wholesale supplier, may stand a slightly greater chance of being infested. But turtles in the wild commonly harbor a startlingly varied group of parasites. You can determine the presence of worms by examining a turtle's feces, since some of the worms are regularly voided. Consult a veterinarian for advice on treatment. Many drugs, known as vermicides, are available to treat the problem. Different drugs are required for different kinds of parasites. The frequency and amount of dosage to be applied varies according to the species of parasite and the size of the turtle.

Worms provide a compelling reason for segregating new turtles, if you're keeping more than one. The parasites, very contagious, will quicly settle in all the turtles in a container. Should you have more than one turtle, and should one of the turtles you've had for some time become ill, whether it be with worms, a cold, a fungus, or any other communicable problem, remove it immediately from the company of its fellows. Give it a warm, clean container of its own, and keep an especially close watch on the other turtles for any symptoms of trouble. A turtle that has been ill should not be returned to a communal habitat until a week has elapsed without any signs of the illness.

Ticks are the most common kind of parasites to afflict the turtle externally, as worms are the most frequent form of internal parasite. Ticks burrow into the skin of the neck, the corners of the eye or mouth, and in the base of the tail. The tick plunges its head into the skin while its body projects above the surface. Appearing as brown or black spots, the ticks are quite noticeable during a close inspection of the turtle. They cannot be allowed to remain, but they cannot be casually removed. If you attempt to pluck them off, using tweezers, you may well get the bodies, but the heads will remain deep in the flesh, and will likely cause an infection.

It is neither costly nor difficult to remove the ticks if you follow the correct procedures. Covering each tick with a thick coat of olive oil will kill it, and kill it quickly. It may fall off or be lifted off with a pair of tweezers. If the tick doesn't want to come, don't keep on tugging. Apply more olive oil, and try again. Cod liver oil or petroleum jelly can also be used to achieve the same result. Whichever you use, be sure to smear it on thickly. After all of the ticks have been removed, apply an antiseptic lotion or ointment to each of the sore spots, and allow it to dry before placing the turtle near water.

The best way to handle any disease is to avoid those conditions liable to cause it. Give your turtle a location that is sufficiently warm and, if at all possible, sunny. Keep the container clean. Don't allow any sort of debris to accumulate. Keep the water fresh. Take special care to supply a varied diet. Give a turtle weekly baths in warm water to which a sulfa solution has been added. Most importantly, make the effort to remain informed about its well-being. Observe its actions with this in mind. Check it regularly for any signs of parasites, both internal and external. Be familiar with the symptoms of colds and other illnesses. And know what to do if such symptoms occur.

Moreover, once again, try to give your turtle an interesting life. Give it a varied environment. Don't force it into cramped, sterile quarters, or into a container devoid of all but the necessities and lacking anything to stimulate or challenge. I can think of no reason to assume that turtles prefer to be bored. In their natural habitats, each day presents them with a variety of challenges, with new and differing occurrences. While you cannot duplicate life in the wild, you can at least give a turtle a spacious and diversified habitat. You can also interact with it. Keeping a turtle isolated from contacts is not wise. The experience of boredom is not limited to humans; nor are its often destructive consequences. Bored animals, melancholy animals, are more likely to become ill. Or, becoming ill, they are more likely to die than animals in a varied environment that duplicates some of the forms of their natural habitats. While species of turtles, and even individuals within species, vary greatly in their reactions to humans, many do seem to enjoy being handled. All of them enjoy a change of locale; individuals kept indoors throughout the winter should be given a chance to wander in the spring and summer—within your sight or within some sort of confines. One family I have read of took their pet tortoise along on picnics. They selected spots well away from any highway. Then around the turtle they ran a long string to which a balloon had been attached. The balloon bobbed gaily several feet above ground. While it did not hamper the movements of the turtle, it allowed the family to easily locate their pet—even in a field of tall grasses.

Keeping more than one turtle will certainly mean more work for you. However, if the turtles belong to the same species, or to species requiring similar conditions, they may prove excellent company for one another, yet another way of alleviating chelonian angst. Of course, you'll have to make a larger habitat for them, and you'll have to spend more money. But if it works, the additional company should work out well for all concerned. It will also provide you with more varied examples of chelonian behavior.

It Followed Me Home

Turtles have probably always been popular with children. But that doesn't mean that turtles collected as pets have always gotten the care they needed. Witness the disastrous history of the baby turtle market and the low survival rate of those millions sold every year. If your child brings a turtle home, or asks you to buy one, you'll have to accept responsibility of seeing that he or she understands the needs of the turtle. And you'll probably have to take a hand in seeing that the turtle's needs are fulfilled. But with your help, a child can successfully tend to a turtle and learn something important about it, and about the need for responsibility in dealing with other living things.

On Turtle Island

There is a rich fund of turtle lore, of turtle tales, of myths concerning turtles. Many of these myths have been developed by native North American and Central American peoples. More complex myths are found in the Far East. Because the turtle was elevated to such a rare position in Japanese, Chinese, and Indian beliefs, I have thought it worthwhile to include some of those myths here, even though China is a long way from the focus of this book. Taken as a whole, the worldwide body of beliefs about turtles, specifically about their spiritual virtues, presents us with an alternative way of looking at and thinking about them. It is my hope that showing how some other societies thought about turtles might stimulate us to reconsider the lowly status now given to chelonians, the indifference or scorn with which they have come to be regarded. Turtles may not be, as some myths have held, companions of the gods; but neither are they the ambulatory automatons society now seems to consider them. There are other ways of thinking about these ancient, shelled reptiles. Some of them follow below.

On a turtle rests the world. This turtle, bearing with dignity the great globe on its broad back, may be aswim in space or floating in the unbroken primal sea. At least, this has been the belief of various simple and complex societies, and has achieved some currency in the world.

The oldest society to have such a myth is that of the Hindus. In their version, Vishnu, second of the three Hindu gods, transforms himself into an immense turtle. Held immovable in space by virtue of his unshakable will, he supports on his back the cosmic vessel in which the gods and demons mix the elements to create the world. Every 4,320,000,000 years the world dissolves, and this churning process must be once again carried through. After the world has been rejuvenated, the turtle remains unalterably in place, supporting now an equally large elephant (or, in some versions, four elephants) upon whom the renewed globe rests.

A myth originating at some unknown date in central Asia also grants the turtle a place as the foundation stone of existence. Before anything else existed, there was a great featureless ocean, and in it an awesomely huge turtle. When this was perceived by the creative power of the universe, the turtle, which had spent its time gazing down into the depths, was turned on its back, and the world was built upon its flat plastron.

The turtle occupied an important position in Chinese cosmology. (Arguably, Chinese beliefs in which turtles occur may have been expressed before the Hindu myths were formulated.) According to at least one version of early Chinese beliefs, the divine tortoise Kwei was the longest-lived of all the supernatural creatures who held some influence over the creation and fortunes of China. It was Kwei who spent 18,000 years directing the formation of the universe, the creation of the earth, and the location of the Moon, Sun, and stars. After these labors were accomplished, Kwei gave life to a line of long-lived turtles by conceiving of them in his thoughts and making the thoughts manifest as being. These turtles were charged to help mankind, pursue truth, and bear the weary burdens of the world. One of them supports India on its back. Another, floating on its stomach, carries the island of paradise on its back. When one of the four pillars supporting the wide universe buckled under the strain, it was one of these turtles that placed itself under the pillar to save the universe.

An actual, but now extinct, species of turtle found in China, the *Pseudocadia anyangensis*, was used in the rites of Chinese priests. Turtle shells were first burned, then examined to determine what messages were carried in the fissures running across the burnt shells. It was claimed that the Supreme Ruler of the universe expressed his edicts to mankind by using such fissures as a sort of chelonian sign language. Moreover, Chinese commentators have in the past claimed that it was out of the readings of divine messages on the shells that written symbols developed. Thus the turtle is also admired as the indirect (but necessary) agent in the Chinese development of a written language. Possibly the religious demands fatally placed upon *Pseudocadia anyangensis* may have been at least partly responsible for the extinction of the species.

Chinese civilization often engendered more than one version of a myth; differing stories of the virtue, importance, and accomplishments of turtles are to be found in various Chinese records. For instance, there is a myth which holds that the original turtle did not so much supervise the making of the universe, but—its shape being the most sublime—actually *became* the universe. In this version, the carapace of the great turtle forms the vaulted sky, the spiritual realm. The interior of the carapace is speckled with stars and reflects their light on the earth. The plastron supports the waters upon which the earth floats. Thus all existence is contained, Noah-like, within a great turtle. The Chinese may have taken the myth literally, or they may have taken it symbolically as an aid to their conceptualization of the universe. It is important to us because it indicates the degree to which Chinese civilization carried the appreciation of turtles. No other society can be said to have paid so much attention to turtles, so greatly identified them with virtue and so readily granted them status as symbols of divine being.

In China a mythical bird figures as the frequent companion of the supernatural turtle Kwei. And in Japan the turtle—regarded as a supernatural symbol of peace, good fortune, and success—is generally pictured in the company of a crane, which stands upon the turtle's shell. In at least one

Japanese legend this partnership is said to have stemmed from the fate of a young couple who fell in love a very long time ago. So deeply in love were they that they transcended the limitations of time imposed on mortals, and lived as loving youths for three hundred years. When they finally perceived what had happened, the "spell" was shattered: the man turned into a turtle, the woman turned into a crane. Together they entered the realm of the godlike beings, and have lived there in companionship ever since. In Japanese myth a tortoise is said to always accompany Benzai-ten, the goddess identified with love, marriage, knowledge, and the gift of eloquence.

According to Engelbert Kaempfer, a German who managed to reach Japan at the end of the seventeeth century, the Ki (or Came) Tortoises, "of all the footed animal produce of the water . . . are most esteemed by the Japanese, being looked upon as peculiar emblems of happiness by reason of the long life which is ascribed to them." Turtles are still kept in pools found on temple grounds, where they are treated with respect and given care so gentle as to allow them to reach advanced ages. In the Far East, including China and, possibly, Japan, it was at one time a popular belief that all turtles were females, and that they reproduced by copulating with snakes. I am at a loss to explain the origins of this belief.

The Mayan civilization of Central America probably comes closest to that of the Chinese in its enthusiasm for turtles. The Mayans had perfected a remarkably complex mathematical system. Thirteen was their sacred number. They kept track of the heavenly bodies and fashioned calendars that stretched backward to the first day of the world and forward to the day of the world's dissolution. Their year had thirteen months. Their native species of turtle had a shell with thirteen sections. This was enough to give the turtle a special status—but there was more. The Mayan civilization depended on agriculture. When the soil in a field was exhausted and more fertile land was needed, farmers would set fire to a part of the surrounding jungle. Seemingly, the Mayans were astonished by the ability of the turtle to survive these fires, to withdraw into the ground and let the fire burn over them, and to emerge un- scathed from the ashy soil. The turtles are said not to have emerged from the ground until after the first life-  giving rains had soaked the soil and made it possible to plant crops. Thus the turtle was most closely identified with rain, with the ability to bring rain, to raise up the crops, and sustain life. Their abilities signaled a super- natural talent for survival. The "slash-and-burn" style of Mayan agriculture, easy but wasteful, may have contributed to the marked internal decline of the Mayas before the conquistadors arrived. The turtle that emerged from the ashes also outlasted those who perceived in it a symbol of divinity.

It is thought that the Mayan system of beliefs granted the turtle a position remarkably similar to that of the Chinese. The Mayans evidently conceived of the sky as being the interior of a turtle's carapace. Rain was admitted through the sky only when one portion (one of the scutes) of the carapace was lifted. In another Mayan legend, the sky is actually a vault held in place by four benevolent figures placed at the four corners of the canopy. One is dressed as an armadillo, another is dressed to resemble a snail, the third is outfitted as a crab, and the fourth as a tortoise.

Bowls and ritual containers in the shape of turtles were created by the Mayans. And, it is thought, even a temple was built to celebrate chelonian virtues. In Mexico at the site of Uxmal, one of the Mayan cities and religious centers, there are the ruins of a temple which features many delicate carv- ings of turtles; conceivably it was built as a shrine for presenting various sacrifices to the turtle spirit. Unlike the Aztecs, the Mayans did not disappear when the wave of Spanish invaders spilled over them. They remained where they were, and are there to this day. Now they dwell in small villages, and lead a simple, often difficult, agrarian existence. Their pronounced regard for the turtle as a symbol of longevity and good fortune no doubt represents some lingering vestige of the ancient Mayan veneration of turtles.

In North America are to be found the greatest number of creation myths in which turtles figure. Curiously, the turtle was not otherwise generally considered an important supernatural figure, as in China. The similarity of their creation tales, as remembered by various tribes, suggests to me a com- mon origin or a process by which myths were passed from group to group, each adding to it the insights of their own particular creative intelligence.

According to the Wyandot Indians, there was a time when both the gods and humans lived above the sky. A group dug one day to get at the roots of a tree, but they dug too far; the tree suddenly sank from sight, falling down through the sky and plunging into the wide and deep ocean that was the world below. It was Turtle who called together a council of all the creatures of the sea, and he who urged that some earth must be brought from the roots of the tree, now in the depths of the ocean, to the surface of the water.

Beaver tried, and drowned. Muskrat dived, and he died too. Otter tried, and Otter drowned. Finally Old Toad reached the sunken tree and, before she died, managed to spit a few droplets of mud onto the back of the turtle. It was enough. From those few bits of soil grew an island on Turtle's back. And then the island grew some more and became the world.

The Iroquois tell the story slightly differently. In their version is a chief, a mean, suspicious, sly man. He and his people lived above the sky in a land illuminated by light given off by the blossoms of a dogwood tree. One day, in a fierce temper, the chief tore out the dogwood tree, creating a hole in the sky. The tree began to die and the light faded. When his wife came to him, she found him lying by the gaping hole, feigning illness. By subterfuge he lured his wife to the hole, then threw her in. As she fell through the clouds, through the sky, the animal spirits of the great watery world beneath debated who should catch her. Turtle was chosen. With the wings of Wild Duck to soften and slow her fall, the chief's wife landed safely on Turtle's great carapace. Beaver, Muskrat, and Otter dived to the bottom of the great waters and brought up the magic earth that had fallen down from the roots of the dogwood tree when it was uprooted. Loon and Bittern spread this earth over Turtle's shell and planted willows in it. As the chief's wife was falling, Fire Dragon had thrust into her hands an ear of corn, and a mortar and pestle. When she woke from her sleep and found land and willow trees about her, she was well pleased. She planted corn in the magic ground, traced furrows for rivers in it, and blessed it, causing it rapidly to increase. But the corn could not grow properly without sufficient light—and the world was very dim. During a second council of animals, it was decided that Small Turtle would ascend the sky to bring back light. Small Turtle succeeded in collecting balls of lightning. She gathered these balls together and tossed them into the sky. The larger ball became the Sun, and the smaller the Moon. Finally, Turtle told Badger and Groundhog to dig holes in the sides of the horizon to allow Sun and Moon to pass through and around the world. In this way day and night came into being.

The Onondaga alter several particulars of the story. In their version, the chief threw his wife out of heaven because he was jealous of her. Loon carried her safely to the back of Turtle, and Muskrat alone brought up soil from the depths to shape a world on Turtle's back.

Again, the Huron version has its differences. In the world beyond the sky in which people once lived, the chief's daughter fell incurably ill. However, one old man known to be wise in such matters told the girl's parents to lay her beside a tree and then to uproot the tree. Everyone set to work with a will; but instead of being uprooted, the tree fell right through, taking with it the girl.

Below the sky was only water. Two swans floated there, and it was they who saw the girl fall from the sky. She was too beautiful to be allowed to drown, so they hurried toward her, catching her and cushioning her great fall. When told of the strange incident, Great Turtle, master of all animals, called a council meeting. Great Turtle told the whole assembly that in his opinion the sudden appearance of this beautiful woman from out of the sky was a good omen. He ordered the animals to search for the tree that had also fallen, and to take from its roots earth which was to be laid on his wide back. The swans showed the other animals where the tree had fallen, and first Otter, then Muskrat, then Beaver, dived for the tree. But the tree was down so far in the dark depths that all who tried failed, and all who failed died. Finally Old Lady Toad said she would try. She was down so very long that everyone thought she too had failed, but were astonished when finally she broke the surface and, before she died, managed to spit out a bit of earth onto Great Turtle's back. Because this was magic earth, it had the ability to grow. And grow it did, into an island, and thence into the world. The swans placed the chief's daughter upon this land. But as the world was still covered in darkness, the animals once again held a council. This time, Great Turtle asked Little Turtle if she thought she could scale the sky and bring back light. She said she would try, and she succeeded, tossing two brilliant balls of lightning into the sky. The first ball was the Sun, the second the Moon. Then Great Turtle commanded those animals who burrowed to dig through into the earth, creating holes in the corners of the sky, so that the Sun and Moon could enter one, go down and then exit through the other. Thus night and day came into being.

This version differs from the others by introducing marital complications into the creation of the world. Sun and Moon were supposed to be man and wife. But they quarreled a lot and were not happy. Once, when Moon passed down into a hole before her husband, he grew angry and beat her violently. Moon fled, and Little Turtle was once again sent to climb the sky to locate her. Little Turtle did so, although Moon was reduced through pining to the size of a thin crescent. Little Turtle helped restore Moon to health, but periodically her husband would mistreat her—which is why she is sometimes seen to have shrunk again to the size of a crescent.

After this a thunder cloud came down. There was rain and a rainbow, a shining bridge along which the deer ran fleetly to find a pasture in the sky. All the other animals saw and envied the deer; Little Turtle, being so compassionate a creature, thus taught them how to climb along the rainbow. And they settled into the sky where they became the stars.

The Delaware Indians have maintained their creation myth in a saga running to 183 verses. While they shared the belief in the world as an island supported on the back of a huge turtle, they added several interesting ideas entirely their own. Their saga, which includes the genesis and migration of the Delaware people, records a time when the tribe takes refuge on the back of a giant turtle during a terrible flood. The story, as it traces the journey of the Delaware through Asia to eastern North America, may possibly indicate that the idea of Great Turtle was originally in circulation in Asia. It has also been asserted (through not proven) that the pictographs in which the Delaware recorded the story are reminiscent of a very early system of Chinese symbols.

That turtle island is possessed of powers greater than anyone can comprehend, and that it cannot safely be abused or taken for granted, is evident in the story the Cheyenne Indians tell about the origins of a pit found in the High Plains region of Oklahoma.

Long ago, before the people had horses, or even metal, forty-nine young men belonging to the same warrior society set out with their chief to hunt buffalo. They walked everywhere, hunting with stone-bladed spears and axes. The hunters walked for many days without seeing any enemies or any game. Finally they turned back, crossing the barren area known as the Staked Plains, to reach their people's camp. No one lived on these plains, for there was little water and stunted bushes. The Sun beat down on the featureless land, and very often there were mirages, patches and even wide lakes of imaginary water, or of mountains, shining far ahead. So when the young men saw something shining brightly in the distance, they did not think  much of it. But this time the object did not recede as they approached it. Indeed, the thing gained in brightness as they came closer, shining, glowing, reflecting the light of the Sun like some mountain of glass. All morning they moved toward the light, for it was in their path, the one they had to travel to reach the next water hole. Some were afraid, some were fascinated, but all went on. All were astonished, when they came to it, to find that the object was a huge water turtle, glistening in the Sun, following a steady pace along the trail to the next water hole. The young men walked alongside the turtle, exclaiming in amazement at its presence. Impetuously, one of them leapt onto its back. Soon another took courage and followed, and then another, and another, until finally only the chief remained walking alongside. He called upon the men to get down, saying that the turtle was a powerful and mysterious force, and should not be trifled with.

Some of the young men tried using their spears to pry the turtle's shell apart, that they might see its great muscles. The turtle, giving no notice to their actions, went on walking at the same steady pace. Others, believing the turtle to be a source of rare power, thought better of such behavior and tried to descend. It was then that they discovered that they were stuck fast to the turtle, and could not move, no matter what they did. Now trembling with fear, they attacked the back and head of the turtle with their weapons, but the stone blades merely shattered, having no effect on the turtle's progress. The young men called out to their chief to save them; he did try to reason with the turtle, promising that if the men were freed they would no longer molest the turtle. And they would indeed honor it always, and would dance the Sun Dance in its memory.

But the turtle gave no sign of hearing, nor did it alter its course or slacken its pace. This continued for some time—the men calling out, the chief running alongside, the turtle plodding on. As the day grew late, it was with horror that the chief perceived the goal of the turtle: a flat body of water, dark, without motion. The young men soon saw it too, and prayed, and cried for mercy. But the turtle walked straight on.

The chief, whose speeches to the turtle had all had no effect, now cried to the warriors, "I have done all I can do, my friends. Something wonderful was shown to you, and you did not respect it. Now you will be punished because you thought wrong in your hearts. I cannot change anything."

"Go home," the young men said, as the turtle moved toward the lake. "Go home, for nothing can be done. Tell our people what happened. Tell our families, and tell them that we will mourn for them. Tell them to mourn for us too." Then the turtle entered the lake.

Up to the last minute, when they were entirely submerged, the young men waved to their chief. Slowly they sank, until the water was up to their chests, then at their chins. Finally only their arms remained above water. Then they too vanished. Soon the water was flat, undisturbed, as if nothing had happened.

The chief returned home alone. And there was a greater grief among the people than they had ever known before. A year later, the entire village packed up and followed the chief to the lake, that they might mourn by its shores. But when they reached the spot where the lake had been, they found instead a great, dry lakebed. In the center of the lakebed was a hole leading into the earth. In it was a great mass of whitened bones. So there the people sat, and there they mourned, for they knew that the bones were the bones of the young men.

The silent turtle of this tale is probably meant to indicate a demon associated with the body of water into which it carries the young men. The Cheyenne believed that each body of water had a particular spirit or demon attached to it. However, the image of the leviathan implacably carrying down into death those who have mistreated or misunderstood it has a wider application. The turtle—and, beyond the turtle, all things living but nonhuman—cannot forever sustain the abuse, the misuse, the disregard with which we are accustomed to treat everything not a part of ourselves. Various strands of the animal kingdom, already greatly weakened, will soon give way, among them some of the over-exploited species of turtle. As each strand snaps, life becomes just that much less rich. And all forms of life to which a failed strand is attached will suffer, becoming unbalanced. Take the turtle as a symbol of nature. Unless we relent, unless we begin to take action to restore life, and not merely take from it, it is conceivable that nature will give way, that the complex processes by which air, water, and food are produced will fail. Stuck immovably on nature's broad back, uncomprehending but finally appalled, we must go down with it into certain collapse. Who then will remain to acknowledge our pale bones?

Ironically, it may be the turtles who will witness and survive our passing—if we go out in one particularly nasty way. Several years ago scientists working for a federal agency fenced off a section of barren desert land. They exposed the land, and thus the small creatures in it, to doses of radioactivity that were gradually increased to levels high enough to simulate the estimated fallout after a war fought with nuclear weapons. Some of the small mammals were badly affected; but most of the insects, and all of the desert tortoises within the enclosure, seemed to come through the experiment unharmed. There is at least the possibility that some kinds of chelonians, the latest versions of a venerable line of survivors, could thus survive even the worst sort of destruction, survive the collapse of *Homo sapiens* as their ancestors survived the extinction of the dinosaurs. It will be a quieter world then, one in which the small creatures of the planet can once again go about their lives unhindered. It could, in fact, be a world somewhat like that imagined as existing *before man* in so many American Indian myths: the kind of fresh world in which miracles of creation are once again possible, and in which Big Turtle floats in the clean sea.

Epilogue

Many years ago, as the people tell the story, a tall white man with a white beard and long hair came from the west, over the ocean, traveling in a boat that moved swiftly without being rowed. Soundlessly his boat drew near the shore of an island off the western coast of Mexico, an island called Tiburon by its inhabitants, the Seri Indians. The island is in the Gulf of California, a body of salt water between the western coastline of Mexico and Baja California. The Seris invited this man ashore. They gave him the name Ahnt ah Koh́-mah, which means "He Who Builds Fires." He went all over the island, stopping at various points, at each stop showing the Seri a different food to eat. In this way did they learn how to kill and eat the sea turtle, deer, jack rabbit, wild pig, fish, crab, shark, sea lion, porpoise, and maguey plant. Before Ahnt ah Koh́-mah taught the Seris how to kill these creatures, and how to prepare fires and cook them, the people had always eaten their food raw; and they had eaten only vegetables, plants, and roots. After he had taught the people these things, and much more, He Who Builds Fires withdrew to the center of the island and entered into the earth, where he remains watching still.

Ever since this man taught them, the Seris say, they have been hunting and eating turtles. They are a small tribe who now live predominantly on the mainland of Mexico, a rough, dry, difficult environment. They have learned, over the centuries, to adapt to a life in which fresh water is hard to get, heat is often severe, and fruits and small game take much effort to secure. However, in contrast to the land, which yields up nourishment only reluctantly, the waters that face the Seris are teeming with life. The Gulf of California, a finger of the Pacific Ocean dividing Baja California from the Mexican mainland, has a unique combination of qualities that make it particularly well suited to sustaining an extremely wide spectrum of creatures. The Seris have always benefitted from, and depended on, this perpetual wealth of life.

They have devoted many of their songs, and much of their folklore, to the creatures they depend on for sustenance. Their relationship with the sea turtle, which they call the *cahuama*, is complex. The Seris not only take the turtles, they respect them and know their habits in a way that only long study can bring about.

> *The cahuama swims on top*
> *Where there is no wind.*
> *When the wind blows he goes down*
> *On the bottom for a long time.*
> *When the wind stops he travels far*
> *Looking for food,*
> *And he eats the seaweed.*

The Seri generally go out in their boats and spear the turtles. At least one species of sea turtle is said to understand the Seri language. After they have speared a turtle, the men will order it to take them home, as their families are waiting for their food. The turtle will obey, pulling the boat toward the shore. Once ashore, the turtle will obediently turn over and expose its neck to be severed. Many tribes of Indians, including the Seris and their neighbors the Pomos, share a certain belief in the powers—in the wisdom and spirit—of animals. According to their thinking, animals are too bright, too powerful, to fall prey, unwittingly, to a hunter. So when an animal is taken, it is because the creature understands that the hunters and the hunters' families must eat. It takes compassion on them. People should thus be grateful to the animals; they should take only those animals they need to survive. The Pomo believe that greed will be punished by the spirits.

The flesh of the sea turtle is eaten. Its shell may be leaned up against the wall of a house to break the force of the wind. The shells are also sometimes used as a sort of percussion instrument during various Seri rituals; half of a turtle's carapace is positioned over a shallow hole, and a dancer beats time upon it. The eggs of sea turtles may also be taken for food whenever a nest is discovered.

The Seris use no more effort than they must in their activities. Centuries of experience have taught them the most efficient and simplest manner in which things should be done. Desert tortoises are taken for specific purposes. When one is needed, it is simply located and turned on its back. Incapable of moving, unable to seek shade, the tortoise soon dies from exposure to the desert sun. Then its flesh is removed and its shell is dried. To make a musical instrument, small stones are dropped into the shell. The shell is then held in two hands, one covering the opening for the neck, the other covering the aperture for the tail. When shaken, it produces a sound like a rattle.

Occasionally marine turtles are left stranded on the beach after the recession of the tide. If one is discovered, men will come and dig a pit for it,

143

allow the pit to fill up with sea water, and keep the turtle there, alive, until a fiesta can be arranged. A dance in which the men participate is held; the turtle and other captives listen to the men sing of the creatures they have killed.

> *The sea comes up*
> *And covers the beach.*
> *The cahuama is left stranded.*
> *I catch him.*
>
> *I dig a pit*
> *To hold the turtle.*
> *It is full of sea water*
> *And no stick holds him.*

It was also a tradition among the Seri that a returning hunter should daub the blood of his catch on his face. If anyone guessed what manner of creature had been killed, the hunter had to share the catch with that person. As the blood of sea turtles looked distinctively dark, the practice of naming and sharing must have been quite frequent; perhaps it encouraged a more equal distribution of a catch.

There are more songs, more turtle lore, from the Seris. All of it is interesting, and some of it is quite powerful and moving. But I have cited from the Seris here for another reason. The Seris, one of the smallest and most simple of Indian tribes, illuminate by their very simplicity a certain attitude, a way of regarding the other creatures of the world with respect.

Many tribes in the Americas have taken turtles. And many of those tribes have also respected, thought about, and made songs about the creatures they took. They did not automatically scorn a creature, simply because they were strong enough or bright enough to kill it. They didn't ignore the world about them.

I'm not suggesting that we begin singing about the animals we use, or even about the natural world we insist on ignoring. But it is highly unlikely that, anytime soon, humans will stop hunting turtles or casually defiling their environments. In the meantime, we can at least encourage others to become familiar with turtles, to see them more clearly, and thus to develop a respect for them and for their successful adaptations to life. Such awareness might help to moderate our use of other creatures. Only after we see a creature clearly—and not as an automaton, a characterless thing—can we begin to respect it. Out of respect will come, hopefully, the desire to moderate our grosser instinct for heedless exploitation. We could not, and should not, pretend to accept the myths and tales of the Seri as fact. But we can, and should, try to grasp the insight animating those tales, for the belief in the worthiness of all creation is not limited to one people, or to one time.

Bibliography

Serious writing on North American turtles has a distinguished history. J. E. Holbrook's *North American Herpetology; or a Description of the Reptiles Inhabiting the United States*, a multi-volume set issued in its complete form in 1842, was the first work to provide careful, complete, scientific descriptions of some of the continent's turtles. The work, which will still repay a careful reading, includes some stunning color plates. Louis Agassiz, perhaps the most famous scientist of mid-nineteenth century America, somewhat updated Holbrook's observations in *Contributions to the Natural history of the United States of America*, released in a four-volume set in 1857. Holbrook and Agassiz each had the virtue of being able to assimilate and represent all the current work in their field in a comprehensive, homogeneous narrative.

While a great amount of valuable research was done on turtles throughout the nineteenth and early twentieth century, it was not until the nineteen-thirties that another encyclopedic work on the chelonians was produced. Clifford Pope, one of the most influential and distinguished of American herpetologists, issued his *Turtles of the United States and Canada* in 1939. A thorough updating of materials on North American chelonians, presented in compact form and writiten with a clear and pleasing style, the volume is still regularly reissued (most recently in 1971) by its original publisher, Alfred A. Knopf (New York). If you want to gather a good, basic library of books on turtles, Pope's book, still a resource of great value, is an excellent first choice.

More recently, two magisterial works on North American turtles are available, and you will need at least one of them for your library. Archie Carr, the dean of modern turtle studies, issued his *Handbook of Turtles: The Turtles of the United States, Canada, and Baja California* in 1952. It is now in its seventh printing, published by Comstock Publishing Associates, a division of Cornell University Press (Ithaca, New York). The *Handbook* collects and applies all relevant facts about North American turtles as of 1952, providing thorough biographies for each of the species and subspecies of chelonians found on the continent. All of this is accomplished in prose that is discriminating and precise, clearly and stylishly written. Archie Carr's complete fascination with turtles is everywhere evident.

Carl H. Ernst and Roger W. Barbour's *Turtles of the United States* was issued in 1972 by the University Press of Kentucky (Lexington). More up-to-date than Carr's book, it incorporates all the research done on turtles since the fifties. Exhaustive in its coverage, it is further distinguished by a portfolio of excellent color photographs, by the number of its black and white photographs, and by a clear, attractive design throughout. The book is a model of what a good scientific work should be. Like Carr, Ernst and Barbour supply extensive bibliographies. I would be hard pressed to choose one book over the other—but if you could get just *one* guide to the study of North American turtles, Ernst and Barbour would have to be it. I own them both.

Bellairs, Angus. *The Life of Reptiles* (2 vols.). New York: Universe Books, 1970. An exhaustive survey of the internal and external structure of reptiles. Somewhat technical, but very complete.

Burn, Barbara, and Emil P. Dolensek. *A Practical Guide to Impractical Pets.* New York: Viking Press, 1976. The most dependable, thorough guide to the keeping of all sorts of animals, including turtles, as pets. Excellent sections on shopping for pets and on the rationale for keeping and caring for them. Specific information on diets and medical care. The only book I've found to discuss what to do with a pet you no longer want and what to do with a decrepit or ailing pet.

Carr, Archie. *So Excellent A Fishe: A Natural History of Sea Turtles.* Garden City: Doubleday & Co., 1973. Another book by the master, concentrating on the lives, remarkable navigational abilities, and present difficulties of the green turtle. Much information is given on the efforts directed by Carr to save and reintroduce the species to its native Caribbean.

Conant, Roger. *A Field Guide to Reptiles and Amphibians of Eastern and Central North America.* Boston: Houghton Mifflin Co., 1975. Excellent field guide, with illustrations in color of each species. Compact enough to carry into the field with you when you go searching for turtles. Also includes brief, informative notes on each species, to enable you to make identifications under demanding conditions.

Ehrenfeld, David W. *Conserving Life on Earth.* New York: Oxford University Press, 1972. An authoritative, grim, and very convincing review of mankind's dolorous effect on wildlife and nature. Only after we understand thoroughly what it is that's gone wrong, and how it happened, can we create appropriate remedies.

146

Froom, Barbara. *The Turtles of Canada*. Toronto: McClelland and Stewart, Ltd., 1976. The only volume I know of devoted just to the turtles occurring in Canada, it is a careful work with a pronounced sympathy for, and understanding of, the chelonians.

Hoke, John. *Turtles and Their Care*. New York: Franklin Watts, Inc., 1970. Although evidently intended for juveniles, this book would amply repay anyone's attention. Concerned only with keeping turtles and tortoises in captivity. Its information on enclosures and diet is superb. This book and the Jocher book are the best sources of information on the *right* way of keeping chelonians as pets.

Jocher, Willy. *Turtles for Home and Garden*. Neptune City, New Jersey: T.F.H. Publications, Inc., 1973. Thorough work on all those matters concerned with keeping chelonians in captivity. Excellent material on enclosures, general care, diet, diseases, and hatching in captivity.

Leutscher, Alfred. *Keeping Reptiles and Amphibians*. New York: Charles Scribners Sons, 1976. Advice by a man with great experience in the field. Especially good on the design of indoor and outdoor habitats.

Pritchard, Peter C. H. *Living Turtles of the World*. Neptune City, New Jersey: T.F.H. Publications, 1967. Very good survey of the entire range of chelonians. Compact but thorough, clear, and interesting. Many illustrations.

Reeves, Martha Emilie. *The Total Turtle*. New York: Thomas Y. Crowell Co., 1975. A concise introduction to the chelonians of the world. Well done, by someone having a deep concern for the future of turtles.

Stebbins, Robert C. *A Field Guide to Western Reptiles and Amphibians*. Boston: Houghton Mifflin Co., 1966. Companion to the Conant volume (described above). Also excellent.

Zappalorti, Robert T. *The Amateur Zoologist's Guide to Turtles and Crocodilians*. Harrisburg, Pennsylvania: Stackpole Books, 1976. A summary of information on North American species. Especially good on those species Zappalorti has studied in the wild, such as the bog turtle. Many color and black and white photographs.

Index

See Table pp. 61–62 for common and scientific names of turtles.

Alabama map turtle. See Plate XI.
Alga(e), 45–46
Alligator snapper, 27, 104
Aquarium, 115-116
Aquatic turtle. See *Fresh-water species.*
    use of term, *xi*
Atlantic green turtle, 33–34
Atlantic hawksbill, 40
Atlantic leatherback, 19–20
Atlantic loggerhead, 33
Atlantic ridley, 33, 41–42, 101
Bog turtle, 46–48
Box turtle, 28–29, 51–53, 128
    ornate, 57
British Columbia, 43
Calcium, 130
    shell development and, 19
Camouflage, 57
Canada, 32, 50
Caretta caretta, 40–41
Central America, folklore of, 135–136
Chelonia mydas, 39-40
Chelonian, use of term, *xi*
Cheyenne Indians, tales of, 139–140
China, mythology of, 134-135
Chrysemys picta dorsalis. See Plate IX.
Chrysemys picta picta. See Plate I.
Chrysemys scripta elegans. See Plate II.
Chrysemys scripta scripa. See Plate V.
Claws, 21–22
Clemmys insculpta, 51–53. See also Plate VII.
Clemmys muhlenbergii, 46–48
Clutch, 32. See also *Nest.*
Colds, treatment of, 128
Common snapper, 104
Cosmetics, from turtle oil, 101
Cotylosaurs, 15-16
Courtship, 28-30
Cryptodira, neck structure of, 21
Cuts and abrasions, 129
Darwin, Charles, 110
Delaware Indians, tales of, 139
Dermochelys coriacea, 38, 42–43
Desert tortoise, 53–57
Diamondback terrapin, 43–45, 102–103
Diet, adult vs. young, 32
Diseases, 126–132
Eastern box turtle, 53. See also Plate XIII.

Eastern mud turtle. See Plate VIII.
Eastern painted turtle. See Plate I.
Egg(s), 30–33, 95–96
"Egg tooth," 31–32
Embryo, development of, 19
Eretmochelys imbricata, 40
Eunotosaurus africanus, 16
Exploitation, 93–110
Eye, inflammation of, 129
Eyesight, 24
Flippers, 19–20, 22, 35, 38
Florida box turtle, 53. See also Plate III.
Florida snapper, 104
Florida softshell, 51
Fresh-water species, as pets, 121-124
    habitats of, 45-51
    locomotion in, 22
    sex life of, 28–30
    soft-shelled, 49–51
Fungus infections, 128–129
Galapagos tortoises, 23, 27, 30, 107–110
Gopher tortoise, 56–57
    as pet, 112
Gopherus agassizii, 53–57
Gopherus berlandieri, 56
Gopherus polyphemus, 56–57
Graptemys geographica, 48–49. See also Plate X.
Graptemys pulchra. See Plate XI.
Green turtle, 39–40, 96–99
Gulf Coast box turtle, 53
Hatchling, 30–33, 35–36
Hawksbill, 33–34, 40, 100–101
Head, mobility of, 21
Hearing, 22
Highways, turtles and, 106–107
Hindus, mythology of, 133–134
Huron Indians, tales of, 138
Incubation, 32
Intelligence, 23–26
Iroquois, tales of, 137
Japan, mythology of, 135
Ki tortoise, 135
Kinosternon flavescens flavescens. See Plate VI.
Kinosternon subrubrum subrubrum. See Plate VIII.
Kwei, 134
Lamina(e), 18, 19
Learning ability, 25
Leatherback, 23, 27, 38, 42–43, 101
Lepidochelys kempii, 41–42
Lepidochelys olivacea, 41–42
Life cycle of turtles. See Plate XII.
Loggerhead, 34, 40–41, 101
Malaclemys terrapin, 43–45

Malaclemys terrapin terrapin, 44. See also Plate IV.
Map turtle, 48–49. See also Plate X.
Marine turtle. See *Sea-going species*.
  use of term, *xi*
Markings, camouflage and, 57
Marshes, 16, 43–45
Mating season, 30
Mayans, folklore of, 135–136
Melville, Herman, 108–109
Mineral supplements, for pet, 117
Miskito, 96–99
Mud turtle, striped, 29–30
Muhlenberg's turtle, 46–48. See also
  Bog turtle.
Myths, 133–144
Nails, 21–22
Neck, head mobility and, 21
Nest, 30–35
North American painted turtle, 28
Northern diamondback terrapin. See
  Plate IV.
Nutrients, of egg, 31
Onondaga Indians, tales of, 138
Ontario, 51
Ornate box turtle, 57–59
Pacific hawksbill, 40
Pacific ridley, 41–42, 101
Painted turtle, 29
"Pancake" turtles, 49–51
Parasites, treatment of, 131
Perception, 23–26
Pills, administration of, 128
Pleurodira, neck structure of, 21
Prairie tortoise, 57–59
Pseudocadia anyangensis, 134
Quebec, 51
Red-eared turtle, 28. See also Plate II.
Respiration, 22–23, 39
Rio Grande turtle, 28
River cooter, 29
Salmonellosis, 113, 126–127
Scales, 21
Scute(s), 19
Sea-going species, conservation of, 100
  exploitation of, 99–101
  habitat and behavior of, 38–43
  hatchlings of, 35–36
  nest of, 34–35
  respiration in, 39
  vocalization in, 23
Seri Indians, 142–144
Sex life, 27–37
Sexual organs, 28
Shell, 16–20

algae on, 46
  sex life and, 27–28
  structure of, 18–19
Side-neck turtles, 21
Skin, 21
Smell, 23
Smooth softshell, 49–50
Snapping turtle, 28, 103–105, 112
Soft-shell (disease), 19, 130
Soft-shelled turtles, 20, 49–51, 104, 112
Southern painted turtle. See Plate IX.
Spine, 18
Spiny softshell, 50–51
Spotted turtle, 29
Stinkpot, 29
"Stem" reptiles, 15–16
Striped mud turtle, 29–30
"Suwanee chicken," 104
Tail, sexual organs and, 28
Taste, sense of, 24
Technology, turtles and, 105–107
Terminology, *x-xi*
Terrapene carolina, 51, 52, 53
Terrapene carolina bauri. See Plate III.
Terrapene carolina carolina. See Plate
  XIII.
Terrapene ornata, 57–59
Terrestrial species, as pets, 118–121,
  habitat of, 51–59
  sex life of, 28–30
  shell of, 20
Terrestrial turtle, use of term, *xi*
Texas tortoise, 56
Three-toed box turtle, 29, 53
Ticks, 131
Tortoise. See also *Terrestrial species*.
  African soft-shelled, 20
  use of term, *xi*
Tortoiseshell, 100–101
Trionyx ferox, 51
Trionyx muticus, 49–50
Trionyx sinensis, 49
Trionyx spiniferus, 50–51
Turtle, use of term, *xi*
Vitamins, for pet turtle, 117
Vivarium, 125–126
Voice, 23
Wood turtle 29, 32, 51–53. See also Plate
  VII.
Worms, in pet turtles, 131
Wounds, treatment of, 130
Wyandot Indians, tales of, 136–137
Yellow-bellied turtle, 28. See also
  Plate V.
Yellow mud turtle. See Plate VI.